ICELAND

TRAVEL GUIDE 2024 – 2025

Explore Iceland's Wonders, Visit Cool Spots, Taste
Yummy Food, and Enjoy Family-Friendly Adventures

Elwood M. Steeves

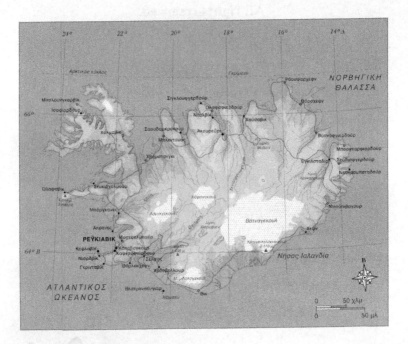

Map of Iceland

Table of Contents

Things to do that you shouldn't miss

Natural Enchantments

Glaciers, waterfalls, and geysers

The Stunning Waterfall Dance

Meetings with Glaciers in Frozen Realms

Geysers: The Steaming Wonder of Nature

Talks with the Glacial Lagoons

The Sounds of Ice Cave Whispers

Hot Springs: A Cozy Welcome from Nature

Protected Areas and National Parks

A Historical Tapestry of Þingvellir National Park

Vatnajökull National Park: Majesty Sculpted by Glaciers

Wonders of the Coast and Mysterious Peaks in Snaefellsjökull National Park

Canyon Marvels at Jökulsárgljúfur National Park

Natural Reserves: Refuges for Peace and Wildlife

Midnight Sun Festival: Never-Ending Daytime Fun

Hot Springs After Dark: Moonlit Swims Under the Stars

Café Culture: Literary Evenings and Thoughtful Discussions

Festivals of Music

Icelandic Airwaves: A Sonoran Investigation of Variety

Uncovered Solstice: Honoring the Midnight Sun

Reykjavik Jazz Festival: Notes That Echo Through the Fjords:

Dark Music Days: An Exploration of Experimental Sounds:

Reykjavik Arts Festival: A interdisciplinary Event Where Music Converges with Other Art Forms:

LungA Art Festival: Community, Creativity, and new Sounds.

INTRODUCTION

This travel guide isn't just about places to go; it's an invite to join a journey where fire and ice create unforgettable experiences.

Picture yourself by massive waterfalls that touch the sky as you flip through these pages. Imagine the Northern Lights, a colorful show lighting up the night sky. Iceland is more than a spot on the map; it's a land full of amazing things waiting for you.

Why Iceland? It's hard to explain, but it pulls in families looking for adventures from hidden villages to ancient ice, and solo travelers seeking peace and romance under the midnight sun. It's where friendly people and chilly surroundings come together, creating a unique blend you won't find anywhere else.

This book isn't just a list of places; it's your key to Iceland's heart. Packed with recommendations and insights, each page opens the door to something extraordinary, making your journey incredible and smooth. It's not just about ticking off spots; it's about truly experiencing Iceland.

Explore the real Iceland beyond standard guides. Join in local activities, chat with the folks, and taste the delicious Icelandic food, each dish telling tales of strength and traditions. Discover the myths about elves and hidden people living by the wild plains and mountains, adding even more magic to your trip.

So, bring this book along as you explore Iceland's personality, history, and diverse landscapes. Iceland has a resilient population, and whether you're a seasoned traveler or it's your first trip, these pages invite you to explore, discover, and fall in love with Iceland's magic.

CHAPTER 1

History of Iceland

Iceland is an island nation in the North Atlantic Ocean, known as the "land of fire and ice." Its interesting past tells a story of being alone, staying strong, and having a unique cultural identity formed over many years.

In the ninth century, brave Norse immigrants, led by Ingólfr Arnarson, first arrived on Iceland's wild coast, marking the official start of the country's history. Seeking a new home and escaping population pressures in Scandinavia, they founded the first settlements and created a society governed by the Althing, one of the oldest legislative assemblies globally.

The challenging landscape influenced life in medieval Iceland. Active volcanoes, glaciers, and unpredictable weather presented difficulties, but Icelanders built a distinct culture based on sagas – epic stories of gods, heroes, and daily life. Passed down orally through centuries, these sagas became the foundation of Icelandic literature.

In the 13th century, the Old Covenant with Norway changed Iceland's fate. Christianity replaced pagan beliefs, but the Black Plague in the late 14th century devastated the population, causing lasting damage to the country's economy and civilization.

Relations with Norway turned into a union with Denmark in 1380, lasting over six centuries. Economic troubles followed due to trade restrictions and natural disasters.

The 18th century brought more challenges with changing weather and economic decline. The Laki volcanic eruption in 1783 led to widespread starvation and agricultural disasters, sparking a growing sense of national identity and interest in Iceland's cultural history.

The 19th century saw Iceland striving for independence. The restoration of the Althing in 1843 was a move towards self-governance. The Kingdom of Iceland was created in 1918 through a union with Denmark, but true sovereignty came in 1944 when Iceland declared itself a republic, breaking away from the Danish monarchy.

Post-war, Iceland found itself caught between East and West, joining NATO in 1951. In the latter part of the 20th century, Iceland transformed from an agricultural to an industrialized nation, using abundant geothermal energy. Fishing became a crucial industry supporting the economy.

In recent years, Iceland gained global attention for environmental sustainability, gender equality, and renewable energy. The country is a leader in progressive government, focusing on ecological sustainability and social welfare.

Through Iceland's history, we encounter a resilient population facing natural and historical challenges. From Viking tales to modern advancements in renewable energy, Iceland's story is one of creativity, adaptability, and a cultural legacy that endures amid the constant changes in the North Atlantic.

Reasons for Traveling to Iceland

Iceland welcomes visitors with a unique blend of wonders spread across its rocky landscape, where nature dances in perfect harmony. This island, like a hidden gem, offers an experience like no other, sitting on the edge of the Arctic Circle.

Iceland is a land of differences. Picture this: huge glaciers alongside volcanic craters, black sand beaches meeting the roaring North Atlantic waves. It's a treat for the senses, a sight to behold. The diverse landscapes showcase the pure, untouched beauty that defines this country.

The Northern Lights, a celestial dance illuminating the Icelandic night sky, are irresistible. With its mesmerizing shades of green and purple, the Aurora Borealis creates a heavenly display that leaves onlookers in awe. It's not just a light show; it's a stunning exhibition of nature's grandeur that stays with you.

Iceland provides a peaceful retreat for those seeking comfort. The timeless landscapes offer a serene atmosphere, encouraging reflection. If you long for a break from the hustle of daily life, the quiet highlands, only interrupted by the gentle whisper of the wind, provide a sanctuary.

Don't overlook the geothermal wonders simmering beneath the surface. Similar to the famous Blue

Lagoon, the bubbling hot springs offer a unique bathing experience that soothes the body and soul. The mineral-rich waters provide a healing haven amidst the surreal surroundings.

Beyond its natural beauty, Iceland is a haven for wildlife enthusiasts. Charming puffins nest on the cliffs, adding a whimsical touch to the coastal views. Seals bask on the beaches, and if you're lucky, you might spot a majestic whale breaking the surface. The abundance of wildlife adds a magical element to the already stunning landscape.

Venturing into the heart of the island reveals its cultural richness. The friendly and kind people of Iceland have a deep connection with their heritage. The tales passed down through the years bring the classic sagas to life. It's an adventure into a world where mythology and reality blend seamlessly.

Food enthusiasts will relish Iceland's cuisine, featuring fresh fish from nearby waters. Icelandic dishes, from hearty lamb stews to the unique flavor of pickled shark, celebrate the natural bounty of the island. And don't miss the delightful treats of Icelandic chocolate.

Adventure awaits all over Iceland. Exploring ice caves is a thrilling experience, leaving a lasting impression with the mesmerizing blue hues of old ice. Glacier trekking challenges the adventurous hiker while offering breathtaking views from the frozen peaks. The awe-inspiring scenery, shaped by the forces of nature, becomes a playground for thrill-seekers.

Iceland stands out, perhaps due to its dedication to sustainability. Everywhere you look, the country is committed to conserving the environment and using renewable energy. It's proof of Iceland's determination to preserve its natural beauty for future generations, making it a destination aligned with the principles of ethical tourism.

Iceland is a captivating journey into the heart of nature, not just a place to visit. You can reconnect with yourself and the planet in this spot where time seems to stand still. Iceland offers an experience beyond the ordinary traveler, whether you aim to witness the elusive Northern Lights, unwind in a geothermal pool, or simply soak in the untamed scenery. So pack your bags and get ready to witness the wonders of Iceland up close.

The weather and the ideal times to go

Iceland is a place where nature decides how life moves, thanks to its interesting yet unpredictable weather. To plan the best times to visit, you need to understand the weather patterns.

Iceland's weather is like a box of mixed chocolates - you never quite know what to expect. It includes wind, rain, sunlight, and even snow, and can change suddenly. This unpredictability adds to Iceland's charm but can sometimes make travel challenging.

Starting with the basics, Iceland has a chilly, moderate marine climate. It doesn't get very hot in the summer or bitterly cold in the winter, but it makes up for that with variety. You can experience all four seasons in a single day.

In the summer months (June to August), the sun seems to never set, giving you long days to explore landscapes lit by the Midnight Sun. Migratory birds fill the air with their songs, and meadows are covered in wildflowers. Summer is perfect for outdoor activities like hiking and road trips.

Autumn (September to November) turns Iceland into a golden paradise. The landscapes transform with earthy colors, and the days get shorter. You might even catch a glimpse of the rare Northern Lights. It's a calmer time with fewer tourists, great for introspective experiences.

From December to February, Iceland becomes a snowy paradise. The whole country looks magical under a blanket of snow, especially during the Northern Lights season. Winter sports enthusiasts can enjoy activities like skiing and snowmobiling.

Spring (March to May) is a time of rebirth. Landscapes wake up from winter, days get longer, and migrating birds return. It's a visual feast with blooming flora and swelling waterfalls creating a symphony of flowing water.

However, Icelandic weather can be erratic. Strong winds and frequent rain are common, and you might experience sunshine, rain, and a breeze all in one hour. This reminds us that nature rules here, adding to Iceland's allure.

Flexibility is key when planning your trip. The best time depends on what you want to see and do. Summer is great for sunshine, winter for the Northern Lights, and autumn/spring for a quieter experience.

Remember, Icelandic weather is more than temperature and precipitation. Pack layers, a waterproof jacket, and sturdy shoes, as the wind can be strong. A warm sweater is a good friend, even in the heat.

Iceland's weather is a mosaic of variables, adding a hint of uncertainty to your journey. Whether you go in summer or winter, be prepared for a wild ride through the weather and enjoy Iceland's natural beauty in all its climatic splendor.

CHAPTER 2

Reaching and Navigating Iceland

Traveling to and through Iceland is like embarking on an adventure through a land of wonders, where every path and road leads to stunning views and life-changing experiences. Let's talk about how to get to this magical island and fully enjoy its beauty.

Getting to Iceland

Arriving by Plane

When you first land in Iceland by plane, the rocky coasts and volcanic scenery create a breathtaking view. The main airport, Keflavík International Airport, greets you warmly amidst the rugged landscape. Immigration and customs procedures are simple, and the staff is helpful and friendly. Buses and taxis are available to take you to the capital, Reykjavík, offering beautiful scenery along the way.

Arriving by Boat

If you arrive in Iceland by boat, you'll be welcomed by an amazing coastal view. Cities like Reykjavík offer a lively atmosphere and convenient transportation options for exploring. Effortless customs and immigration procedures ensure a smooth entry. Stepping off the ship, the cool Icelandic air greets you, and buses and taxis are easily accessible from the dock. With English widely spoken, there's little language barrier, making your arrival easy. Travel directly into the heart of Icelandic adventure, exploring the country's natural beauty and rich cultural heritage.

Traveling Through Iceland

Driving

Driving is a common way to get around due to well-maintained roads that wind through various landscapes. Renting a car is like having your own magic carpet, taking you to secluded waterfalls, geysers, and other rural treasures.

Coaches and Buses

Buses and coaches act like chariots, transporting you across the island if you prefer someone else to drive. The bus system connects major towns, providing a relaxed and scenic mode of transportation. With someone else handling the roads, it's like having a rolling window to Iceland's natural beauty.

Within-country Travel

Domestic flights act like wings, taking you from one area of the island to another for those wanting to cover more ground quickly. Imagine flying above glaciers and volcanoes, making Iceland's vastness feel smaller. Domestic flights give access to remote locations, turning the entire island into your playground.

Cycling and Climbing

Now, imagine a slower pace, where hiking boots and bicycles become your reliable companions. It feels like you're dancing to the rhythm of Icelandic nature when exploring on foot or by bicycle. You can stop whenever you like to take in the view, making it a personal opportunity to get to know the area.

Ridesharing and Taxis

Taxis and rideshares act like personal chauffeurs in towns and cities. When you need a ride to a specific location or just want a break from driving, they're available. It's an easy way to navigate cities without worrying about parking or finding your way.

In Iceland, getting around offers a variety of options. Each mode of transportation adds a unique touch to your Icelandic vacation, whether you're flying domestically over glaciers, driving the Ring Road in a rented vehicle, or enjoying the scenic landscapes by coach. Now hop on board, go, and let the adventure unfold across this incredible country.

CHAPTER 3

Organizing Your Iceland Vacation

In this chapter, we'll help you plan your trip to Iceland, providing useful tips and essential details to ensure a smooth and unforgettable vacation. Let's start the planning process together, taking care of everything from pre-trip preparations to packing suggestions and selecting the perfect accommodation, ensuring each step brings you closer to the wonders of Iceland.

Pre-trip Necessities

Getting ready for your Icelandic vacation is like gearing up for an incredible journey into a land of wonders. There are important things to consider before setting foot on the volcanic soil to ensure your journey goes as smoothly as possible.

1. Travel Documents and Visa

Think of your travel documents and visa as the keys to the kingdom of Iceland. Ensure your passport is ready for the trip, like a well-traveled buddy. Check if you require a visa to make your arrival into Iceland as smooth as a well-practiced dance.

2. Immunizations and Well-Being

Consider vaccines as an expedition-worthy cloak for your trip. Confirm the status of routine immunizations and, if necessary, consider getting additional shots. It's like insurance against unforeseen medical difficulties, allowing you to travel across Iceland comfortably.

3. Travel Insurance

Consider travel insurance as your safety net, there to save you in unforeseen circumstances. It functions similarly to a trustworthy buddy, covering lost belongings, medical emergencies, and canceled trips. Having travel insurance ensures you're prepared for anything that may arise, like having a supporting presence.

4. Money and Planning

Think of Icelandic krona as your traveling friend, assisting you in navigating the local economy. Learn about the Icelandic krona and budget like a cautious captain navigating a ship. It's similar to ensuring you have the necessary supplies for an amazing trip.

5. Clothes and Weather

Imagine yourself as an intrepid traveler ready to face the weather. Check the weather forecast and pack accordingly for Iceland's unpredictable climate. It's like having emergency weather gear ready to go, . ensuring you're comfortable no matter what Mother Nature throws at you.

6. Essential Items

Consider necessary items as a portable toolbox for any situation. Don't forget to bring a camera to capture moments, a reliable bag, and comfortable shoes. It's similar to preparing for a treasure hunt—making sure you have everything you need to maximize your time in Iceland.

7. Language and Culture Etiquette

To connect with the people, think about learning a few Icelandic words and phrases. It's like shaking hands with new individuals and building relationships. Learn about cultural etiquette so that your interactions flow like a harmonic dance, honoring the customs of this special place.

30 Icelandic Expressions for Easy Communication

•Hi there, Halló

•Góðan daginn says "good morning," "good afternoon," and "good evening" to Gott kvöld.- Góða nótt - Good nightKindly, Vinsamlegast

•Many thanks - Takk fyrir

•Thank you so much - Þú ert velkominn/velkominPlease pardon me, AfsakiëNo - Nei; Yes - Já;I apologize. Ég er leið/Íreytur.What's your name? - Hvað heitir þú?

The name Ég Heiti is my name.What's up with you? Is it true that þú það?

• Goodbye - Bless ~að bara gott, þakka Íér fyrir I'm alright, thank you

• In what location is...? What is...?

•What is the price of this? What does þetta cost?

• Are you fluent in English? - Talar þú ensku?

• I'm not sure - Ég skil ekki • Assistance! - Hjálp! • Cheers! (during toasting): Skál!; Water: Vatn; Food: Matur; Need help: Ég Íarf aðstoð; Restroom/bathroom: Klósett/sturtur; I'm lost: Ég er tapað/ur tapað/Íreytur; Where can I get a taxi? - Hvar ég en styrke leigubíl?

• Is WiFi available here? - Is WiFi still in use?

8. Emergency Contacts and Communication

Think of emergency contacts as your lifesaver, always ready to lend a helping hand. Keep a list of important numbers and share your travel plans with a family member or trusted friend. It's like having a safety net that keeps you connected, even in the most remote areas of Iceland.

These preparation essentials are like the foundation of your Icelandic adventure. They ensure you're ready for the journey ahead, allowing you to fully enjoy the wonder and beauty of Iceland. So, get yourself prepared, gather your excitement, and start counting down to your Icelandic adventure!

Getting Ready for your trip Iceland
Packing Tips for Iceland Adventure

Getting ready for Iceland is like preparing for a thrilling journey to a land with diverse landscapes and experiences. Imagine the weather as you pack – from windy days to sudden sunny spells – to ensure you're ready for whatever surprises this Nordic paradise may have in store.

1. Layered Clothing

Think of your clothes as layers of weatherproof defense. Put on thermal underwear, add a waterproof jacket and sweaters. It's like building a barrier that adjusts to Iceland's changing weather, keeping you warm and ready for discovery.

2. Water-Resistant Gear

Consider your waterproof trousers and jacket as dependable allies against sudden downpours. Think of them as a barrier to keep you dry as you explore glaciers, waterfalls, and other natural wonders.

3. Sturdy Footwear

Think of your footwear as reliable allies, ready for Iceland's varied terrain. Choose durable, waterproof boots for muddy routes and rough terrain. Your boots will see you through every step, like dependable wheels.

4. Gloves and Hats

Consider your hats and gloves as indispensable friends, shielding you from the chilly Icelandic wind. It's like wrapping yourself in a warm hug to keep your limbs toasty, especially in winter. Pack them – they're small but powerful shields against the cold.

5. Daypack and Backpack

Imagine your bag as a trustworthy travel partner, holding necessities as you discover Iceland's treasures. It's like a smaller assistant ensuring you have everything for an exciting day. A daypack is perfect for shorter outings.

6. Binoculars and Camera

Think of your camera as a wonderful tool ready to capture Iceland's beauty. It's like stopping time to preserve memories of scenic landscapes. Binoculars are like your eyes, enhancing the excitement by helping you see animals and distant sights.

7. Power Adaptor

The secret to keeping your gadgets charged is your power adaptor. It ensures your phone, camera, and devices are operational – a magic wand for communication. Pack it in your luggage, a small but essential gadget for your Iceland trip.

8. Personal Items

Consider your personal belongings, like medicine and toiletries, as small luxuries from home. It's like bringing a bit of your home life to Iceland. Stow them in a bag, a treasure box of necessities to make you feel at home abroad.

Packing for Iceland is like assembling a kit for a big journey. Each item serves a purpose, guiding you through the pleasures and challenges of this magical place. Envision the experiences ahead, and let the packing process be a prelude to the amazing voyage about to begin.

CHAPTER 4

Choosing the Right Accommodation

Choosing where to sleep in Iceland is like uncovering the key to a pleasant and comfortable journey. After a day of exploring the attractions of this enchanting country, we'll guide you through various lodging options in this chapter to help you pick the best place to rest and rejuvenate. Get ready to explore the best accommodation choices for your Icelandic vacation, from cozy guesthouses to rustic cabins.

Accommodations

Choosing the perfect hotel for your stay is like finding the perfect spot in a vast, welcoming world. It's not just about having a bed and a roof; it's about feeling at home in a new place. Let's explore the simple yet essential aspects of selecting the right hotel, a decision that can make your vacation truly memorable.

First things first: the location.

Think of it like choosing a neighborhood. Do you want to be in the heart of the action, with lively markets and bustling streets around you? Alternatively, you might prefer a quieter spot, away from the city hustle, where you wake up to the sounds of birds. Consider the surroundings that make you feel most comfortable.

Now, let's talk about the budget. Hotels come in various sizes and styles, and their prices vary widely. Think of it like selecting a dish from a menu: there's something to satisfy every appetite. Regardless of your budget or willingness to spend a bit more for added comfort, there's a hotel out there that's perfect for you. It's about finding the right balance between affordability and comfort.

Next up are the amenities. Think of it like choosing ice cream toppings. Do you prefer a hotel with a spa, pool, or gym for added relaxation? Some hotels offer breakfast as a pleasant perk to start your day. Others may have a cozy lounge where you can read and unwind. Consider the small things that can enhance your overall enjoyment of the visit.

The friendliness of the staff is another key factor. It's like having friendly neighbors next door. A kind word from the concierge or a warm welcome at the front desk can make a significant impact. A welcoming staff contributes to making you feel more at ease in your home away from home.

Now, let's keep it simple when it comes to the size and style of the room. Are you traveling with family, as a couple, or solo? Think of it like choosing the right size jacket: not too big, not too small. Whether you prefer a spacious suite or a cozy single room, there's accommodation that suits your needs.

Consider reviews, much like getting recommendations from friends before trying a new restaurant. Reading about others' experiences gives you an idea of what to expect. Keep it straightforward: positive reviews often indicate satisfied customers, and a string of compliments is like a reassuring pat on the back for your chosen hotel.

Think about the hotel's ambiance, similar to creating a playlist for a journey. Decide if you'd like to be in a lively place perfect for socializing or a more tranquil setting for some quiet time. The atmosphere sets the right tone for your preferences and enhances your stay.

Accessibility is crucial. Is the hotel conveniently located near the areas you want to explore? It's like choosing a hiking trail. Pick a place based on your preferred mode of transportation, whether it's walking, using public transportation, or taking a taxi.

Lastly, let's discuss uniqueness, much like selecting a book to read. Every hotel has a unique story. Whether it's a charming old building with interesting architecture or a place with a quirky theme, look for a hotel that appeals to you because of its distinct character.

Choosing the perfect hotel involves similar considerations to choosing a travel companion: compatibility, comfort, and a sense of community. It's more than just a place to stay; it's about establishing a temporary home that enhances your overall trip experience. So, go ahead and pick the accommodation that feels like the right fit, and embark on your adventure knowing that your stay will be as memorable as the experiences that await you.

Guesthouses

Choosing the perfect guesthouse for your visit is like discovering a hidden gem in a sea of options. Finding a place to sleep is crucial, but it's also about uncovering a spot that feels like a home away from home—a comfy corner to relax after a day of exploring. Let's explore the simple yet vital factors that will help you pick the ideal guesthouse for your trip.

Firstly, consider the location. Think of it as choosing a tree to enjoy a beautiful day under. Do you prefer being in the heart of the action, surrounded by the town's hustle and bustle? Alternatively, maybe you're attracted to a quieter area, away from the main streets, where the sound of birdsong can be your morning soundtrack. Consider the type of environment that would suit you best.

Now, let's talk about the budget. Like snacks in a market, guesthouses come with different price tags. Consider what comfortably fits in your pocket. There's a guesthouse waiting to welcome you, regardless of your budget; some are modest and cozy, while others are ready to spend a bit more for extra comfort. It's about finding the right balance between affordability and comfort.

Amenities, like small treats, can add to the enjoyment of your visit. Do you want a guesthouse with a shared kitchen for basic meals? Some may offer a shared lounge, like a common living area, where you can meet fellow travelers. Others may have a garden, like having your own private green haven. Think about what little things can make your stay more enjoyable.

Talking about staff, they are like reliable, pleasant neighbors. A warm greeting at the front desk or a helpful suggestion from the owner can put you at ease right away. Kindness goes a long way in making your visit cozy and enjoyable. Your stay at the guesthouse will feel more like a homecoming when the staff provides a personal touch.

Consider the size and style of the room. Are you traveling as a group, a couple, or solo? Like well-fitting shoes, guesthouses come in various sizes. There's a room type that works for you, whether you prefer a private room or don't mind sharing a space like a dorm.

Reviews, those brief stories from other visitors, are like postcards from friends who have been there before. Reading about others' experiences gives you insight into the ambiance and quality of service. Keep it short; positive reviews often indicate satisfied customers, and a series of kind remarks is like a comforting pat on the back for the guesthouse of your choice.

Think about the guesthouse's atmosphere. It's like choosing music for your trip: do you want a lively place to meet new people, or a more relaxed environment for some alone time? The atmosphere sets the mood for your visit according to your preferences.

Like picking a trail for a nature walk, accessibility is important. Is the guesthouse conveniently located in relation to the places you want to visit? Choose a place that suits your preferred mode of transportation, whether it's walking, using public transportation, or hailing a cab.

Lastly, let's discuss uniqueness. Like books on a shelf, every guesthouse has a unique history. Maybe it has a special theme that makes your stay more interesting, or it's a historic structure with wonderful elements. Look for a guesthouse that captures your interest with its own charm.

Choosing the perfect guesthouse involves similar considerations to choosing a travel partner: compatibility, comfort, and a sense of community. It's a decision that goes beyond simple lodging; it's about creating a makeshift sanctuary that enhances your entire trip experience. So, go ahead and choose the guesthouse that feels like the right fit, and embark on your journey knowing that your stay will be just as memorable as the experiences that await you.

Hostel

Choosing a hostel for your trip to Iceland is like picking a lively hub that values simplicity and friendship. Let's explore these qualities, picturing why hostels are a great choice for your Icelandic adventure.

Hostels offer a budget-friendly option without compromising on essentials, making them akin to cozy havens for budget-conscious travelers. It's like finding a comfortable spot that saves money for exploring Iceland's wonders. Opting for a hostel means selecting affordable accommodation without sacrificing the basic amenities.

Envision the common areas of a hostel as vibrant town squares, filled with diverse visitors from around the world. It's like receiving an open invitation to socialize, share stories, and make new friends. If you seek the companionship of fellow travelers, hostels are the perfect choice due to their lively atmosphere.

Consider the dorm-style rooms as cozy havens where comfort and simplicity go hand in hand. It's like having a private space within a shared living environment. After a day of exploring Iceland, rest in the comfortable bunk beds that resemble small nooks.

Hostel kitchens can be seen as shared food play areas where guests cook as a large family. It's like having the flexibility to prepare your favorite dishes while enjoying Iceland's beautiful scenery. The common kitchen area fosters camaraderie around the dinner table.

Hostels can be thought of as strategic outposts, often located in convenient spots offering quick access to Iceland's top attractions. It's like having a home base that minimizes travel time, allowing you to maximize your exploration of breathtaking landscapes, charming villages, and waterfalls.

Consider hostels as flexible havens that easily adapt to last-minute changes in your travel plans. It's like having adjustable reservations that offer convenience and assurance as your schedule changes. Hostels' flexibility is an open door inviting serendipity to join your Icelandic journey.

Regard hostel staff as friendly tour guides, ready to provide travel tips and insider knowledge. They offer recommendations for must-see places, local cuisine, and hidden gems, much like knowledgeable friends. Staying in a hostel provides access to a wealth of local information, ensuring you experience Iceland beyond what travel guides show.

Hostels can be compared to housing chameleons, offering various room options to suit different group sizes and preferences. Hostels cater to a range of traveler needs, whether it's a private single room or a sociable shared dorm.

Choosing a hostel in Iceland is like selecting a vibrant and social base for your travels. The affordable mindset, communal spaces, and diverse housing options encourage memories and connections. Picture the lively atmosphere of a hostel stay amidst Iceland's stunning landscapes, where simplicity meets friendship.

Hotels Made of Ice

Choosing an ice hotel for your trip to Iceland is like embarking on a magical journey into a snowy paradise.

With dazzling ice crafted into the very walls around you, ice hotels are like frozen wonders. Being surrounded by the glimmering beauty of frozen art is like stepping into a storybook. The magical ambiance created by the ice makes your visit special and unforgettable.

Think of the ice hotel's design as a collection of sculptures, where each room is a masterpiece carved from snow and ice. It's like living in an ice art exhibition, with intricate patterns and dreamlike motifs showcasing the skill and creativity of the artists. It feels like entering a crystalline dream at every turn.

Picture your ice bed as a warm, cozy cocoon with fur and layers of insulation to keep you warm. It's like snuggling up in a chilly retreat while breathing in the pure, crisp winter air of Iceland. The sleeping bags are snug and warm despite the cold, much like comforting blankets.

Consider the ice decorations in the hotel as a magical light show. The ice sculptures illuminated by soft, ethereal lights create a scene resembling a frosty firefly dance. The walls themselves seem to glow, creating a serene and captivating atmosphere.

Think of your accommodations as a series of cozy igloos, a separate sanctuary within the ice hotel. It's like having your very own frozen haven, with controlled interior temperatures that strike the perfect balance between the comforts of a warm refuge and the freezing cold outside.

Imagine the themed ice suites as immersive experiences, each using frozen details to narrate a unique story. You feel like you've stepped into an ice dreamscape or winter wonderland, surrounded by imaginative designs that transport you to another realm. Staying in one of these suites is like being in a one-of-a-kind work of art, with every little detail contributing to the overall story.

Consider the ice bars and restaurants as cool dining spots where even the drinks are served in ice glasses. It's like dining in a frosty palace while enjoying the carefully sculpted surroundings. The ice bars offer a chilly yet enjoyable retreat, akin to a frozen oasis.

Think of the ice hotel as a central hub for winter activities, providing experiences like snowshoeing, ice carving, and even witnessing the northern lights. It's like having an icy playground of frozen delights right outside your door. These extra thrilling activities ensure that the frosty surroundings become a canvas for adventure, adding even more excitement to your stay.

Choosing an ice hotel in Iceland is like opting for a once-in-a-lifetime opportunity, where your accommodation captures the essence of winter. The frozen marvels, sculpted architecture, and unique experiences create a visit that is both enchanting and unforgettable. Envision the chilly allure of an ice hotel, where each moment is like a scene from a frosty novel, all set against the breathtaking backdrop of Iceland's wintry landscape.

Frm Stays

Opting for a farm stay in Iceland is like delving deep into the natural beauty and simple charm of the country.

In Iceland, staying on a farm is akin to relishing the peace and calm of the countryside. Picture waking up to the serene melody of the countryside and the gentle sounds of nature surrounding you. It's like discovering a peaceful retreat away from the hustle, allowing you to connect with the land and its tranquil rhythm.

Envision a farm stay as the gateway to a genuine Icelandic adventure. It's like stepping into the daily life of a local, witnessing agricultural tasks, and fully immersing yourself in the rich tapestry of Icelandic culture. A farm stay provides an authentic taste of living a true Icelandic life away from the crowds of tourists.

See your accommodation as a welcoming farmhouse, where you're always met with warmth and simplicity. It's like entering a comfortable home away from home, complete with snug rooms and tasteful yet modest decor. The farmhouse is a cozy haven where you can relax after a day of exploration.

Consider farm stays as places where hearty, home-cooked meals are the norm. It's similar to enjoying wholesome, affectionately prepared Icelandic cuisine. Picture yourself at a table filled with local specialties, savoring dishes that embody the essence of genuine Icelandic hospitality.

Think of the livestock as your friendly neighbors. It's like having a community of feathered and furry companions that add charm to your travels. Interacting with the animals, whether petting horses, observing lambs, or simply spending time with these gentle friends, is a delightful pleasure.

Imagine waking up to breathtaking views outside your window. A stay at a farm is like being surrounded by stunning scenery, such as meadows and rolling hills. It's a visual delight that enhances the beauty of your Icelandic adventure, providing a serene yet awe-inspiring backdrop.

Consider the farm owners as gracious hosts who extend authentic Icelandic hospitality. It's akin to visiting friends eager to share their love for the region and its traditions. Their warm greetings are like a friendly embrace, elevating your farm stay beyond mere lodging.

Think of a farm stay as a starting point for outdoor experiences. It's like having a playground with hiking, horseback riding, and nature trail exploration just outside your door. The farm's surroundings become your personal exploration zone, with activities that serve as mini-chapters of your Icelandic journey.

Choosing an Icelandic farm stay is akin to opting for a special blend of comfort, authenticity, and rural tranquility. Every element, from the welcoming farmhouse accommodations to the gracious hospitality of the farm owners, works together to provide a memorable and enlightening experience. Envision, therefore, the serenity of a farm stay, where the picturesque Icelandic landscape becomes an integral part of your travel adventure.

Host Airbnb

Opting for an Airbnb when visiting Iceland is like choosing a comfy spot you can truly call your own. Let's dive into the cozy details that make Airbnb a welcoming choice for your trip.

Staying in an Airbnb feels like returning home. Picture yourself in a cozy space with all the warmth of a beloved home. It's akin to finding a retreat where you can unwind after a day exploring Iceland's beauty.

Think of your Airbnb as a window into local life. It's like sharing a space with a local friend. The furniture, decor, and personal touches offer a unique and authentic experience that goes beyond typical tourist spots, giving you glimpses into Icelandic life.

Consider your Airbnb kitchen as a cooking haven. It's like having the freedom to prepare meals just like you do at home. The kitchen serves as a versatile space for your culinary adventures, whether you're brewing your morning coffee or cooking a simple Icelandic dish.

Imagine the bedrooms as your private havens. Each room provides a sense of seclusion and comfort, like having your own retreat amidst Iceland's stunning landscapes.

Think of your Airbnb host as a helpful and friendly guide. They act as supportive friends, offering tips and recommendations tailored to the area. These suggestions are like a treasure map leading you to the heart of Iceland's culinary delights, from the best local cafes to hidden gems off the usual tourist path.

Booking an Airbnb reservation is like having a flexible plan. It's similar to having choices that match your travel schedule, whether you're staying for a short or long time. Airbnb ensures your lodging suits your needs.

Consider Airbnb features as familiar comforts. It's like having a cozy living room, a garden, and maybe even Wi-Fi. These touches make your stay more pleasant, turning your Airbnb into a snug corner amidst Iceland's vast landscapes.

Think of the privacy Airbnb provides as a valuable treasure. It's like having a personal space where you can relax without interruption. Being independent allows you to set your own pace and itinerary, giving you the freedom to tailor your Icelandic experience.

Choosing an Airbnb in Iceland is like claiming a bit of the local lifestyle for yourself. Every aspect of the accommodation—from the inviting atmosphere to the unique local touch and personalized spaces—contributes to a comfortable, friendly, and distinctly you stay. Picture yourself unwinding in your cozy Airbnb as the breathtaking scenery of Iceland unfolds just outside your door.

CHAPTER 5

Iceland's Outdoor Adventure Activities

Explore the heart of Iceland's natural beauty on an exciting adventure in this chapter on outdoor activities and adventure. Get ready to discover the many opportunities to fully engage with the spectacular outdoors of this Nordic paradise, from stunning views to heart-pounding activities. Whether you love nature or seek adventure, Iceland has an experience waiting for you. So buckle up, and let the outdoor adventures begin!

Trails for Hiking and Trekking

Imagine embarking on an adventure through Iceland's pristine, wild beauty, where each step feels like a dance with the natural world. In this realm of fire and ice, hiking and trekking are more than pastimes—they're immersive experiences that connect you to untamed landscapes.

The air is crisp with the smell of dirt and moss as soon as you step onto the pathways. It's like entering a painting, with Iceland's wildness as the canvas. The paths lead to hidden delights like meandering lanes through a woodland straight out of a fairy tale.

The variety of Icelandic landscapes is captivating. It's like turning pages in a photo album, unveiling a new marvel at every bend. Trekking through slopes filled with wildflowers may make you feel like you've discovered a hidden garden. The gentle slopes create a calming cadence, resembling the undulating waves of an emerald sea.

As you climb, the view changes, similar to ascending a ladder to the heavens. The scenery transforms into wide plateaus where the wind tells ghost stories from long ago. Being alone in the unspoiled beauty of nature is a powerful and humbling experience.

The pathways in Iceland resemble complex webs, linking you to magnificent waterfalls dropping like silver threads. A symphony of running water creates a nature-inspired live show. Meeting other hikers on the trails is like encountering kindred souls traveling together, sharing admiration for the endless vistas.

Animals, like puffins and seals, may be your companions on the trails. Puffins soar across the skies or perch on rocks like protectors of the shore. Seals greet you along the shoreline, their heads bobbing in the water, eyes wide with curiosity.

Iceland's routes are not always easy, with rocky trails and river crossings testing your fortitude. Every stride feels like conquering a little obstacle, giving you satisfaction that enhances the whole experience.

After exploring, there are hot springs, nature's warm hug, like discovering a secret oasis. Surrounded by

Icelandic landscapes, it's a peaceful time to decompress and reflect.

The pathways may lead to a campground at day's end. Imagine creating your little sanctuary in the natural world. Tent camping under a starry sky and storytelling over a campfire represent a return to the fundamentals of human existence.

Hiking in Iceland caters to all skill levels, with trails for experienced hikers seeking challenges or novices enjoying leisurely strolls. It's a choose-your-own-adventure tale resulting in different revelations.

Hiking in Iceland is like flipping through the pages of an old story the country has written. The trails convey cultural legacy, geological past, and the spirit of a people sculpted by nature. Keep in mind that the trip itself is more important than the final objective. It's about taking in a country's beauty and being invited to share its narrative. Every step is like painting a new picture with memories lasting long after you've left the trails behind.

The Laugavegur Path

Imagine traveling through the central region of Iceland, where the scenery unfolds like the pages of a book. The Laugavegur route is not just a trail; it's a beautiful tapestry of nature that leaves a lasting impression on all who walk its paths. It's often called a hiker's paradise.

Picture starting your walk in Landmannalaugar, where the hills seem to dance with color. The geothermal wonders paint the soil in red, orange, and yellow hues, creating a surreal backdrop. The Laugavegur Trail welcomes you with nature's vibrant strokes, as if entering a painting.

The trail winds through vast valleys filled with wildflowers, like an ancient path carved into Icelandic terrain. It feels like strolling through a meadow where blooms, reflecting Iceland's vivid summer, sway in the light breeze. The pure scent of the untouched wilderness fills the air.

With each climb, the scenery transforms. The hills provide endless views in all directions, like silent sentinels. Standing on the edge, it feels like watching Iceland unfold before you. Being free amidst untouched beauty is both invigorating and humbling.

Like a storyteller, the Laugavegur Trail weaves glacier legends into its narrative. Imagine approaching the massive glaciers, like enduring sentinels. The glacial tongues shape the landscapes, creating a breathtaking display. It's like reaching a masterpiece created by nature, where time seems to stand still.

The river crossings become an adventure along the trail. Picture jumping from rock to rock and crossing streams that meander over valleys. Take a soothing break, dipping your toes in the clean Icelandic streams, reflecting the surroundings like liquid diamonds.

The Laugavegur Trail's huts offer a unique experience, serving as cozy retreats in nature's grandeur. It's like finding a haven, where tired trekkers gather to laugh and share tales. The rustic cabins against the wild backdrop enhance the journey, a return to essentials and a reconnection with life's basics.

Don't forget the hot springs, nature's warm embrace after a day of exploration. Think of it as finding a secret oasis in the wilderness. Like a natural spa, the calming waters provide a chance to unwind and reflect on the day's events. Surrounded by Icelandic landscapes, it's a serene time.

Like any good book, the Laugavegur Trail is full of unexpected turns. The weather changes suddenly, much like a character in a tale. One moment the sun caresses your cheeks, the next clouds form, and the sky turns gray. It's a reminder that the trail is just a backdrop for nature's ever-changing drama.

Along the Laugavegur Trail, meet other hikers like characters in a book, each with their tale. Conversations exchange stories of adventures and wonders, flowing like the rivers across the valleys. The companionship enhances the sense of community during the trek, an unspoken agreement among hikers.

With its diverse views, the Laugavegur Trail is a visual delight changing with each step. It's like flipping through the pages of a travel book filled with illustrations of glaciers, flower-filled meadows, flowing waterfalls, and geothermal wonders. Every element deepens the experience, weaving a mosaic of memories.

Like a teacher, the trail imparts lessons about gratitude and resilience. The challenging terrain, with steep ascents and rocky paths, tests your resolve. It's like conquering small obstacles and feeling a sense of accomplishment that enhances the whole experience. Learn to enjoy the journey, live in the moment, and find beauty in nature's simplicity on the Laugavegur Trail.

As the Laugavegur Trail concludes, the midnight light casts a pink and gold haze over the sky. The surroundings take on an otherworldly hue, like a dream. Witnessing the climax leaves you in awe of the everlasting enchantment of Icelandic summer evenings, akin to viewing a heavenly masterpiece.

The Laugavegur Trail is a journey through Iceland's soul, not just a hiking spot. It offers you a chance to be part of a story that the land itself is writing. Every step on your journey is like painting a new picture, memories that last long after leaving the trail behind. More than a route, the Laugavegur trail is a chapter in Iceland's history, and as you travel its paths, you become a valued part of that history.

Fimmvorduhals Pass

Fimmvörðuháls Pass is more than a trail; it's an adventure through views that bring thoughts of the natural world's grandeur. Let's embark on an adventure that lets you be part of Iceland's captivating story.

Entering Fimmvörðuháls Pass feels like stepping into a world where nature reigns supreme. The trek begins at Skogafoss, a powerful waterfall roaring like distant thunder. It's like the start of an exciting journey, with cool mist from the falling water welcoming you.

The path takes you through various landscapes, much like an old trail etched into Icelandic soil. Imagine it as a route winding through fields of wildflowers, their vibrant colors against rolling hills. The fresh air carries the scent of earth and murmurs from nearby rivers.

The scenery unfolds as you ascend, like turning the pages of a novel. It's like climbing stairs to the sky, each step revealing a new view of Iceland's natural wonders. Valleys cradle nature's beauty, both fleeting and enduring, like open arms. It's an expedition into the wild interior, where the land proudly displays its ancient scars.

As a great storyteller, Fimmvörðuháls Pass guides you through the realm of glaciers. Picture it as a stroll toward icy giants, timeless keepers. The glaciers shape landscapes with their ice tongues, creating a beautiful and humble sight. It's like approaching nature's cathedral, where profound stillness speaks volumes.

Crossing rivers becomes a playful dance with nature on Fimmvörðuháls Pass. Think of it as leaping from rock to rock, spanning glistening streams. The water invites you to pause and appreciate the simplicity of untouched Icelandic streams, reflecting the surroundings like liquid jewels.

The route leads through volcanic landscapes, akin to walking through a living artwork. It's like stepping into a fantastical world where molten rock and flames beneath your feet tell a story. Like old calligraphy, volcanic scars give the pathway a unique texture, reminding of Iceland's geological dance with the elements.

Meeting fellow travelers, kindred souls on this shared journey, happens on Fimmvörðuháls Pass. Conversations flow like rivers, laughter resonating in the Icelandic environment, and tales being exchanged. The companionship enhances the sense of community during the trip, like an unspoken agreement among hikers.

Huts along the route provide a unique experience, like warm shelters amidst nature's majesty. It's like finding a haven where hikers gather to share tales, warmth, and the pure joy of being surrounded by wild beauty. Amidst the Icelandic environment, the little cottages become a refuge and a home away from home due to their simplicity.

Fimmvörðuháls Pass weather is a character of its own, casting shifting hues across the sky. Perhaps the sun kisses your face one moment, then clouds form, creating gray patterns the next. It's a reminder that nature controls the pace, and the route is a canvas for her ever-changing artistic vision.

Accompanying you on Fimmvörðuháls Pass is wildlife. Puffins, enchanting seabirds, may soar through the air, their wings sweeping across wild terrain. Approaching the coast, seals may wave, their curious eyes watching passing tourists. It's like meeting creatures in a wild realm where all contribute to the Icelandic story.

As the day progresses, the pink and gold hues of the midnight sun paint the sky. The surroundings take on an otherworldly hue, like a dreamscape. Witnessing the climax leaves you in awe of the everlasting enchantment of Icelandic summer evenings, akin to viewing a heavenly masterpiece.

Fimmvörðuháls Pass is a chapter in Iceland's vast narrative, not just a trail. This journey invites you to be part of a story that the land itself is writing. Every step you take on your journey is like painting a new picture with memories that last long after you've left the path behind. Fimmvörðuháls Pass is not just a pass; it's an adventure into Iceland's spirit, and as you traverse its trails, you become a valued character in that story.

Tours of puffins and whale watching

First, picture yourself on a boat for a once-in-a-lifetime whale-watching experience, with the wind blowing through your hair. It's like going on a mission to see peaceful ocean giants, whales, gracefully dancing under the waves. The boat cuts through Icelandic seas like a reliable horse, leaving a path of excitement behind.

The water seems like a huge canvas ready to reveal living masterpieces as you look out to sea. Spotting a whale's spout is an exciting experience, akin to finding buried treasure. It reminds you that you're a visitor in the aquatic world of these amazing creatures and gives you chills.

The size of whales, those ocean giants, reveals the mysteries of the deep. They breach and dive, like a ballet with enormous creatures moving elegantly. Their exhalations create a melody, a rhythmic symphony across the ocean waves.

Don't forget the dolphins, those joyful aquatic acrobats. Think of it as a show where these energetic animals jump and spin in the boat's wake, seemingly performing just for you. It's like an invitation to a happy dance, a celebration of life in the open.

Seabirds guide you across the marine realm. Fulmars soar gracefully, capturing the sea wind with their wings. Kittiwakes provide a chorus to the ocean's symphony with their characteristic sounds. These feathery companions remind you that the ocean is a thriving environment full of life.

Now, let's focus on puffins, those adorable seabirds with brightly colored beaks. Taking a puffin tour is like a voyage to their coastal homes, where these cute animals live in busy towns on cliffs. It's like entering a seabird city, where puffins go about their lives in a whimsical manner.

The cliffs, like tall buildings, house puffin colonies resembling active communities. It's like a cityscape where these little bird inhabitants stroll around, adding charm to the wild coastal environment. With their black and white outfits, puffins look like stylish city dwellers.

Observing puffins shows their social dynamics, similar to a bustling town plaza. Puffins have courting behaviors, like a lovely dance, telling romantic tales with the sound of breaking waves and seaweed in the air. With expressive looks, these seabirds seem to tell stories about life along the coast.

Puffin colonies on ocean rocks offer stunning vistas. It feels like standing on the edge of the earth, with ocean air kissing your face and seabirds calling around you. The views capture the spirit of coastal splendor, like a postcard come to life.

Seeing puffins in their natural environment is like looking into a busy market where each bird has a specific role. Nesting burrows become cozy homes, and cliffs become gathering spots for puffins. Their simple existence against the wild outdoors reminds you of the beauty of life in its basic form.

The journey resumes aboard the whale-watching boat. Whether it's humpback whales, minke whales, or elusive orcas, the water tells its tales. Each sighting adds nuance to the story of your marine trip, like a chapter in a maritime novel. The ocean becomes a vast library of underwater stories with its secrets and wonders.

Memories of puffin excursions and whale viewing resonate like notes in a nautical symphony as the boat returns to the harbor. It feels like the end of a journey that took you from the ocean's depths to the top of coastal cliffs. During your Icelandic journey, water, with its legends of whales and puffins, becomes a valued aspect.

So, fellow explorer, don't miss the chance to cruise the wide seas in Iceland. Take a puffin and whale-watching cruise to witness the sea's narrative unfold before your eyes. On this voyage, the water is the narrator, and you, dear traveler, are the captivated audience.

Climbing Glaciers and Investigating Ice Caves
It feels quiet and peaceful when you step onto the ice. The snow under your feet makes a comforting sound,

like a lullaby, and the air is fresh. The glacier in front of you looks like a wide white plain, inviting you to go on a cold adventure. It's like walking on a frozen canvas with winter's colors painting the area in shades of blue and white.

Hiking on glaciers is like dancing with a huge ice giant. It's an expedition where every step needs careful navigation on the changing glacier surface. Walking on ice, surrounded by towering frozen peaks, is both humbling and thrilling. It's like temporarily moving to a frozen realm.

The ice beneath your feet, like any living thing, carries marks from time. The glacier has traces of earlier times in its layers of packed snow. It's like reading a book about the history of glaciers, with each layer telling the story of past snowfall turning into crystalline ice.

As you reach the glacier, expansive views open up like a magnificent painting. The nearby mountains guard the frozen terrain like friendly sentinels. It feels like you're entering the Arctic region, with chilly winds carrying tales from the far north. The glacier, stretching beyond your sight, is a tribute to the majesty of nature.

Now, let's explore the ice cave at the center of this icy wonder. Think of it like entering a crystal-clear church. The blue ice walls of the cave seem to shine from within, creating the image of a shimmering haven. It's like stepping into a secret room where the glacier's majesty is fully exposed.

Discovering the ice cave is like stepping into a time-warp secret universe. The smooth, flowing contours of the ice walls create an otherworldly atmosphere. It's like being surrounded by a sea of perfectly preserved waves, each ripple frozen in time. An optical symphony plays as the light reflects off the transparent ice.

The soft blue color of the ice adds a touch of mystery to the cave, like a soft whisper. It feels like being surrounded by chilly tones that inspire awe and serenity. The ice's ability to absorb and refract light creates an ethereal environment. A silent moment of reflection in the center of the glacier's icy embrace.

Some formations in the ice cave resemble frozen sculptures. Imagine discovering an art exhibit in nature, where each piece of ice is a work of art shaped by time and temperature. The warm light catches the ice stalactites, resembling crystalline chandeliers.

The echoes inside the ice cave produce a strange melody, like whispering from the glacier itself. The sound of your footsteps mixed with the occasional trickle of melted ice creates a soft tune. The cave's quiet and serene atmosphere invites you to pause and contemplate the wonders of nature.

Exploring ice caves and trekking on glaciers is like an enthralling dance with nature. Immersing yourself in a frozen world that reveals its secrets to the brave is like accepting the frigid embrace of winter. The glacier becomes a playground for those seeking the unadulterated beauty of the Arctic because of its enduring existence.

The memories of the cold experience linger like ice kisses on your cheeks as you leave the glacier. The brisk winds seem to bid you farewell, carrying stories of icy terrain. The glacier becomes a treasured chapter in your Arctic adventure with its majestic peaks and secret ice tunnels.

So, fellow explorer, if you ever find yourself in Iceland's freezing embrace, don't miss the chance to explore ice caves and hike on glaciers. On this adventure, the icy terrain transforms into your playground, and the glacial treasures reveal themselves like pages from a wintry fairy tale. Enter the Arctic region, where the glacier becomes your guide, and let your own icy journey be shaped by the legends of ice and snow.

CHAPTER 6

Iceland's Outdoor Adventure Activities

Embark on an adventure to explore Iceland's natural wonders in this chapter on outdoor activities and adventure. Get ready to discover the numerous opportunities to fully engage with the splendid outdoors of this Nordic paradise, from breathtaking views to thrilling activities. Whether you love nature or seek excitement, Iceland has an experience waiting for you. So, get ready, and let the outdoor adventures begin!

Trails for Hiking and Trekking

Imagine going on an adventure through Iceland's untouched, wild beauty, where each step feels like a dance with the natural world. In this land of fire and ice, hiking and trekking are more than just hobbies – they are immersive experiences that connect you to the untamed landscapes, creating a sense of ancient and eternal connection.

The air is cool, carrying the scent of earth and moss as you step onto the paths. It's like entering a painting, with Iceland's wildness as the canvas. The trails lead you to hidden treasures, like winding paths through a woodland straight out of a fairy tale.

The variety of Icelandic landscapes is fascinating. It's like flipping through a photo album, with each turn revealing a new wonder. Trekking through green slopes filled with vibrant wildflowers might make you feel like you've found a secret garden. The gentle slopes create a calming rhythm beneath your feet, resembling the undulating waves of an emerald sea.

As you climb, the view changes. Think of it like climbing a ladder to the sky. The scenery becomes vast plateaus where the wind whispers ancient stories. Being alone in the untouched beauty of nature is a powerful and humbling experience.

The paths in Iceland resemble intricate spiderwebs, connecting you to magnificent waterfalls cascading like silver threads from cliffs. The sound of running water creates a symphony as you hike. It's like being at a live show where nature takes the spotlight, surrounded by such natural beauty.

Don't forget the glaciers – massive ice formations that seem to defy gravity. These frozen giants are reached via trails, resembling veins on the Earth's skin. It's like approaching a sleeping giant, where every nook and cranny holds a history spanning eons. The glaciers silently observe the ever-shifting terrain.

Meeting other hikers on the trails is like encountering kindred spirits on a shared journey. There's a silent understanding of mutual appreciation for the endless vistas, creating a strong sense of camaraderie. Conversations flow like streams, sharing stories and suggestions for the next amazing sight.

Hiking in Iceland isn't always easy, with rocky trails, river crossings, and steep climbs testing your resilience. But each step is like overcoming a small obstacle, bringing a sense of satisfaction that enhances the entire experience.

After a day of exploration, there are hot springs – nature's warm embrace. Imagine finding a hidden oasis in the middle of the wilderness. Like a natural spa, the soothing waters offer a chance to unwind and reflect on the day's events. Surrounded by Iceland's unspoiled beauty, it's a peaceful time.

As the day ends, the paths may lead you to a campground. Picture creating your own sanctuary amidst nature's majesty. Tent camping under a starry sky and sharing stories around a campfire represent a return to the basics of human existence.

Hiking in Iceland is accessible to explorers of all skill levels. Whether you're an experienced hiker seeking off-the-beaten-path challenges or a beginner enjoying a leisurely stroll with stunning views, there's a trail for everyone. It's like a choose-your-own-adventure story, where each option leads to a different revelation.

Hiking in Iceland is like flipping through the pages of an old story written by the country itself. The trails convey the cultural legacy, geological history, and unwavering spirit of a people shaped by nature's forces, much like chapters in an epic novel.

So, remember that the journey is more important than the destination as you lace up your boots and hit the Icelandic trails. It's about embracing a country's pure beauty and being invited to share in its narrative. Every step on your journey is like painting a new picture with memories that will last long after you've left the trails behind.

The Laugavegur Path

Picture exploring the heart of Iceland, where the scenery unfolds like the pages of a simple storybook. The Laugavegur route isn't just a path; it's a canvas of natural beauty that leaves a lasting impression on everyone who walks its trails. Some call it a paradise for hikers.

Imagine starting your walk in Landmannalaugar, where the hills seem to dance with colors. The geothermal wonders paint the soil in red, orange, and yellow, creating a unique backdrop. The Laugavegur Trail welcomes you with the vibrant colors of nature, like entering a painting.

The path winds through wide valleys filled with wildflowers, like an old trail carved into the Icelandic land. It feels as if you've stepped into a meadow where the flowers, reflecting Iceland's lively summer, sway in the light breeze. The fresh smell of the wilderness, the scent of the ground, fills the air.

As you climb, the view changes. There are endless sights in every direction, provided by the hills, like silent guards. It feels like you're on the edge of the world, observing Iceland unfold before you. Being free and surrounded by untouched beauty is both invigorating and humbling.

Similar to a storyteller, the Laugavegur Trail weaves glacier tales into its narrative. Imagine approaching massive glaciers that stand like enduring guards. Like frozen rivers, the glacier edges shape the landscapes, creating a breathtaking sight. It's like arriving at a masterpiece crafted by nature, where time seems to stand still.

The river crossings become an adventure as you follow the trail. Picture hopping from rock to rock and crossing streams that wander through the valleys. You can take a relaxing break, dipping your toes in the clean Icelandic streams, reflecting the beauty like liquid diamonds.

The huts along the Laugavegur Trail offer a unique experience, acting as cozy shelters amidst nature's grandeur. It's like finding a haven where tired trekkers gather to share laughs and stories. The rustic cabins against the wild backdrop add to the charm. It's a return to basics and a reconnection with life's essentials.

Don't forget the hot springs, nature's warm embrace after a day of exploration. Imagine stumbling upon a secret oasis in the wilderness. Like a natural spa, the soothing waters let you unwind and reflect on the day's events. Surrounded by Iceland's unspoiled beauty, it's a peaceful time.

Similar to a good book, the Laugavegur Trail is full of unexpected twists. Like a character in a story, the weather can change suddenly. One moment the sun may warm your face, and the next, clouds may form, and the sky turns gray. It's a reminder that the trail is just a stage, and nature is the real creator of the ever-changing drama.

Along the Laugavegur Trail, you'll meet other hikers, like characters in a book, each with their own story. Conversations flow, sharing tales of adventures and wonders seen along the way, like rivers cutting through valleys. The companionship enhances the sense of community during the trek, almost like an unspoken agreement among hikers.

With its diverse views, the Laugavegur Trail is a visual treat that changes with each step. It's like flipping through a travel book with illustrations of glaciers, meadows, waterfalls, and geothermal wonders. Each element deepens the experience and creates a mosaic of memories.

Similar to a teacher, the trail teaches lessons about gratitude and resilience. The challenging terrain, with steep ascents and rocky paths, tests your determination. It's like overcoming small obstacles and feeling a sense of accomplishment that enriches the whole experience. You learn to appreciate the journey, live in the present, and find beauty in the simplicity of nature on the Laugavegur Trail.

As the Laugavegur Trail concludes, the midnight light bathes the sky in pink and gold hues. The surroundings take on an otherworldly appearance, like a dream. Experiencing this climax leaves you in awe of the everlasting enchantment of Icelandic summer evenings, akin to witnessing a heavenly masterpiece.

The Laugavegur Trail is a journey through Iceland's spirit, more than just a hiking trail. This journey invites you to be a part of a story written by the land itself. Every step on your journey is like creating a new picture with memories that will stay with you long after you've left the trail behind. Beyond being a route, the Laugavegur route is a chapter in Iceland's story, and as you travel its paths, you become a cherished part of that story.

Fimmvorduhals Pass

Fimmvörðuháls Pass is more than just a path; it's a journey through landscapes that inspire thoughts of the beauty of the natural world. Let's embark on an adventure that lets you be a part of Iceland's captivating tale.

Walking on Fimmvörðuháls Pass feels like entering a world where nature reigns supreme. The trek begins at Skogafoss, a powerful waterfall that sounds like distant thunder. It's like starting an exciting journey, with the refreshing mist from the falling water welcoming you.

The trail takes you through various landscapes, like an old path etched into the Icelandic earth. Imagine it as a route winding through fields of wildflowers, their colors a vibrant symphony against the rolling hills. The air carries the scent of soil and the gentle sounds of nearby rivers.

As you ascend, the scenery unfolds like the pages of a book. It's like climbing steps to the sky, revealing new views of Iceland's natural wonders with each step. The valleys cradle nature's beauty, fleeting yet enduring, like outstretched arms. It's an expedition into the wild interior, where the land proudly displays its ancient scars.

Similar to a skilled storyteller, Fimmvörðuháls Pass guides you through the realm of glaciers. Picture it as a stroll toward icy giants serving as timekeepers. The glaciers shape the landscapes with their frozen tongues, creating a sight that is both beautiful and humble. It's like approaching nature's cathedral, where the silence speaks volumes.

Crossing rivers becomes part of the journey on Fimmvörðuháls Pass. Think of it as a playful dance with the natural world, leaping from rock to rock across glistening streams. The water invites you to pause and appreciate the simplicity of untouched Icelandic streams, reflecting the surrounding beauty like liquid jewels.

The trail leads through volcanic landscapes, akin to a journey through a living artwork. It's like entering a fantastical world where molten rock and flames beneath your feet tell a story. Like ancient calligraphy, the volcanic scars give the path a unique texture, a reminder of Iceland's geological dance with the elements.

As you traverse Fimmvörðuháls Pass, you encounter fellow travelers – kindred souls on this shared journey. Conversations flow like the many rivers, laughter echoing in the Icelandic environment as tales are exchanged. The companionship enhances the sense of community during the trip, like an unspoken agreement among hikers.

Huts along the route provide a unique experience, like warm shelters amidst nature's grandeur. It's akin to finding a haven, a place where hikers gather to share stories, warmth, and the pure joy of being surrounded by wild splendor. Amidst the Icelandic environment, these little cottages become a refuge and a home away from home due to their simplicity.

The weather on Fimmvörðuháls Pass is a character itself, casting changing hues across the sky. One moment the sun may warm your face, and the next, clouds form gray patterns. It's a reminder that nature dictates our pace, and the route is a blank canvas for her ever-changing artistic vision.

Accompanying you on Fimmvörðuháls Pass is wildlife. Puffins, enchanting seabirds, may soar through the air, their wings sweeping across the wild terrain. As you approach the coast, seals may wave to you, their curious eyes observing passing tourists. It's like meeting characters in a wild realm where all creatures play a role in the Icelandic story.

As the day progresses, the pink and gold hues of the midnight sun paint the sky. The surroundings take on an otherworldly hue, like a dreamscape. Experiencing this climax leaves you in awe of the everlasting enchantment of Icelandic summer evenings, akin to witnessing a heavenly masterpiece.

Fimmvörðuháls Pass is a chapter in Iceland's vast narrative, not just a route. This journey invites you to be a part of a story that the land itself is writing. Every step you take on your journey is like creating a new picture with memories that will last long after you've left the path behind. Fimmvörðuháls Pass is more than a pass; it's an adventure into Iceland's spirit, and as you traverse its trails, you become a valued character in that story.

Tours of puffins and whale watching

To start, imagine yourself sailing on a boat for a special whale-watching experience, feeling the wind in your hair. It's like going on a mission to find calm ocean giants, the whales, gracefully dancing beneath the waves. The boat moves through the Icelandic seas like a dependable horse, leaving a sense of anticipation behind.

As you gaze out to sea, the water seems like a vast canvas waiting to reveal its living masterpieces. Spotting a whale's majestic spout is an exciting moment, like discovering a hidden treasure. It reminds you that you are a guest in the aquatic world of these incredible creatures, sending chills down your spine.

The sheer size of whales, those huge ocean creatures, reveals the mysteries of the deep. They leap and dive, resembling a ballet with graceful movements that defy their size. The sound of their breath creates a melody echoing across the ocean waves, like a rhythmic symphony filling the air.

Don't forget the dolphins, those playful aquatic acrobats. Picture it as a show where these energetic animals jump and spin behind the boat, as if performing just for you. It's like an invitation to a joyful dance, a celebration of life in the open sea.

Seabirds join you on your journey, acting as guides in the marine realm. Fulmars soar gracefully, their wings capturing the sea breeze. Kittiwakes add their characteristic sounds to the ocean's symphony. These feathered companions serve as a natural wink, a reminder that the ocean is a vibrant environment full of life.

Now, let's focus on the puffins, those adorable seabirds with brightly colored beaks. Going on a puffin tour is like exploring their coastal homes, where these cute birds live in busy towns on cliffs. It's like entering a seabird city, where puffins go about their daily lives in a whimsical manner.

The cliffs, like tall buildings, host puffin colonies resembling active communities. Picture it as a cityscape where these little bird inhabitants stroll around, adding a touch of charm to the wild coastal environment with their humorous antics. With their black and white attire, puffins look like stylish city dwellers.

Watching puffins reveals their social dynamics, much like a bustling town plaza. Puffins engage in courting behaviors, akin to a lovely dance. It's like witnessing a romantic story unfold with the sound of breaking waves and seaweed in the air. With their expressive looks, these seabirds seem to share stories about life along the coast.

The puffin colonies, perched on ocean rocks, offer stunning views. It feels like standing on the edge of the earth, with the ocean breeze on your face and seabirds calling around you. The scenery perfectly captures the essence of coastal beauty, like a postcard coming to life.

Observing puffins in their natural setting is like watching a busy market where each bird has a specific role. Nesting burrows become cozy homes, and the cliffs serve as gathering places for puffins. Their simple existence against the wild outdoors reminds us of the beauty of life in its most basic form.

Back on the whale-watching boat, whether it's humpback whales, minke whales, or elusive orcas, the water, like a never-ending storyteller, shares its tales. Each sighting adds a layer to the story of your marine journey, like a chapter in a sea novel. The ocean becomes a vast library of underwater stories, full of secrets and wonders.

The memories of puffin adventures and whale watching resonate like notes in a maritime symphony as the boat returns to the harbor. It feels like the end of a journey that took you from the ocean's depths to the top of coastal cliffs. During your Icelandic adventure, the water, with its stories of whales and puffins, becomes a cherished part.

So, my fellow explorer, don't miss the chance to cruise the wide seas if you ever find yourself in Iceland. Take a puffin and whale-watching cruise to witness the sea's story unfold before your eyes. On this voyage, the water acts as the storyteller, and you, dear traveler, are the captivated audience.

Climbing Glaciers and Investigating Ice Caves

It feels peaceful when you step onto the ice. The snow under your feet makes a comforting sound, like a lullaby, and the air is fresh. The glacier in front of you looks like a wide white plain, inviting you on a chilly adventure. It's like walking on a frozen canvas with winter colors in shades of blue and white.

Walking on glaciers lets you explore the frozen landscape, like a gentle dance with the colossal ice giant. It's an expedition where every step is careful on the changing glacier terrain. Walking on ice, surrounded by towering frozen peaks, is humbling and exciting. It's like temporarily being in a frozen world.

The ice beneath your feet shows marks from time, with layers of packed snow revealing remnants of earlier times. It's like reading a book on the history of glaciers, where each layer tells the story of past snowfall turning into crystalline ice.

The vast views when you reach the glacier are like a magnificent painting. The nearby mountains protect the frozen land like friendly guards. It feels like entering the Arctic, with chilly winds carrying tales from the far north. The glacier, stretching beyond your vision, is a tribute to the majesty of nature.

Now, let's explore the ice cave, the heart of this icy wonder. Think of it as entering a crystal-clear church. The blue ice walls shine from within, creating a shimmering haven. It's like stepping into a secret room where the glacier's majesty is fully revealed.

Discovering the ice cave is like entering a time-warp secret universe. The ice walls' smooth contours create an otherworldly atmosphere. It's like being surrounded by a sea of perfectly preserved waves, each ripple frozen in time. The light in the cave reflects off the transparent ice, creating an optical symphony.

The ice's soft blue color makes the cave more mysterious, like a soft whisper. It feels like being surrounded by chilly tones, inspiring awe and serenity. The ice's ability to absorb and refract light creates an ethereal environment. A silent moment of reflection in the center of the glacier's icy embrace.

Some formations in the ice cave resemble frozen sculptures. Imagine finding an art exhibit in nature, where each piece of ice is shaped by time and temperature. The warm light catches the ice stalactites, resembling crystalline chandeliers.

The echoes inside the ice cave produce a strange melody, like whispers from the glacier itself. Your footsteps and the occasional trickle of melted ice create a soft tune. The cave's quiet atmosphere invites you to pause and contemplate the wonders of nature.

Exploring ice caves and trekking on glaciers is like an enthralling dance with nature. Immersing yourself in a frozen world that reveals its secrets is like accepting winter's frigid embrace. The glacier becomes a playground for those seeking the unadulterated beauty of the Arctic.

The memories of the frigid experience stay with you like ice kisses as you leave the glacier. The brisk winds seem to bid you farewell, carrying stories of icy terrain. The glacier becomes a treasured chapter in your Arctic adventure with its majestic peaks and secret ice tunnels.

So, fellow explorer, if you ever find yourself in Iceland's freezing embrace, don't miss the chance to explore ice caves and hike on glaciers. On this adventure, the icy terrain becomes your playground, and glacial treasures reveal themselves like pages from a wintry fairy tale. Enter the Arctic region, let the glacier guide you, and shape your own icy journey with the legends of ice and snow.

CHAPTER 7

Romantic Vacations for Two

This section provides the perfect mix of adventure, tranquility, and nature to create lasting memories with your special someone. Let Iceland be the backdrop for your romantic getaway, complete with the dancing Northern Lights, secluded hot springs, and charming coastal villages. Join us as we uncover the secrets of a romantic journey in the heart of this extraordinary location.

Romantic Spots for Couples & Hidden Retreats
Embarking on a quest to discover Iceland's most romantic spots and secret getaways is like opening the door to a world where love and nature coexist. Picture being surrounded by the elegance and simplicity of these private places with your significant other.

Private Hot Springs for Two

Imagine finding secluded hot springs away from the hustle and bustle. Picture the tranquility and warmth of the ocean embracing both of you. The sounds of bubbling geothermal waters surround you as you enjoy peaceful moments in these secret havens, resembling nature's own sanctuaries.

Coastal Peace at Vik's Black Sand Beach

Exploring the black sand beach in Vik becomes a romantic adventure. Imagine walking hand in hand along the coast, your love story serenaded by the rhythmic waves. Your footsteps become a tribute to a shared journey etched in the beauty of the shore, and the black sands resemble a canvas.

Intimate Waterfall at Seljalandsfoss

Entering Seljalandsfoss, the whispering falls, feels like discovering a haven for lovers. Imagine feeling the mist kiss your faces as you stand behind the falling water curtain. The water's symphony provides a backdrop for your special moments at the falls, which are like nature's love poetry.

The Midnight Sun Above Snaefellsjökull

Witnessing the midnight sun set over Snæfellsjökull is like participating in a heavenly dance. Imagine the golden light filling the air around you as you welcome the endless day. Your romantic hideaway beneath the glacier is bathed in a warm tint, like an endless daybreak.

Ballet of the Northern Lights at Thingvellir

Seeing the Northern Lights dance above Thingvellir is like attending a space ballet with your sweetheart. Imagine the ghostly lights painting the night sky above the ancient settings, creating a heavenly display. The lights resemble a dance that you both participate in, a celestial celebration of your love.

Cozy Evenings in Log Cabins

Rustic cabins become a warm retreat for special occasions. Imagine the simplicity of being together in the peaceful outdoors, the crackling fireplace, and sharing stories. The cabins are like nests of love, where warmth comes from shared moments as much as the fire.

Gullfoss Lookout Picnic

At Gullfoss Lookout, a picnic becomes a romantic rendezvous with a view. Imagine lying on a blanket beneath the imposing waterfall with the Icelandic sky above you. A picnic is akin to a gourmet exploration, with the richness of your shared experience reflected in the tastes of local fare.

Charm of a Coastal Village in Stykkishólmur

Stykkishólmur's charming seaside town atmosphere is like strolling through a dreamy novel setting. Imagine charming streets, vibrant homes, and a picture-perfect atmosphere by the sea. The town invites you to immerse yourself in its allure and create memories with your significant other, similar to a romantic retreat.

Helicopter Flights above Volcanoes

Picture the helicopter gracefully soaring over Iceland's untamed landscape as you take off hand in hand. Below, craters, lava fields, and historical formations reveal the grandeur of volcanic eruptions. Imagine yourselves as protagonists in your own romantic tale, set against the striking backdrop of Iceland's natural wonders.

Gazing Upon Geothermal Wonders

Imagine seething mud pots below and steam gushing from secret hot springs as the chopper flies above these geothermal wonders. The vistas provide a unique romantic adventure, similar to a visual symphony of Earth's powers. Together, you and your companion witness the wonders of nature, marveling at Iceland's thermal riches as a pair.

Setting Foot on Distant Volcanic Peaks

Imagine the helicopter softly descending into secluded volcanic peaks to offer a quiet time amid Iceland's unspoiled nature. It's like entering a private stage just for the two of you, where the majesty of the volcanic terrain serves as a blank canvas for your love to grow.

Toasts to Champagne Against a Stunning Panorama

Imagine taking in the breathtaking scenery of Iceland while sipping a champagne toast as you land at a panoramic vista. The breathtaking background becomes a testimony to your shared joy and celebration, while the bubbling effervescence reflects the excitement of your love adventure.

Helicopter Serenade at Sunset

Imagine a helicopter sunset serenade as the day comes to an end. Warm tones paint the volcanic terrain beneath the sun's golden rays as it sets, creating an unparalleled romantic atmosphere. It's a moment frozen in time, where the everlasting beauty of an

Icelandic sunset is reflected in the love you have for your sweetheart.

Starry Nights and Volcanic Shadows

Imagine the chopper ascending once more as dusk descends, this time beneath a canopy of stars. The enigmatic shapes of the volcanic forms underneath emerge against the deep blackness of the Icelandic night. It's like traveling through a romance tale set in space, with the stars serving as witnesses to your enchanting journey.

A helicopter flight above Iceland's volcanoes is more than just an adventure; it's a romantic symphony against this unique country's breathtaking geological features. Every moment becomes a new chapter in your love story, where the splendor of Iceland's volcanic landscapes blends with the excitement of adventure. So, go above and beyond with your romantic retreat, and let the helicopter trip become a cherished memory of romance and discovery.

Iceland's romantic spots and secret hideaways are more than just travel destinations—they're milestones in your romantic journey. Every moment adds to the canvas of your journey together against Iceland's breathtaking scenery. Let these undiscovered treasures be the backdrop for your enchanting journey, as love blossoms amid the enchantment and simplicity of this remarkable region.

CHAPTER 8

Adventures That Are Family-Friendly

Get ready for a trip filled with joy and discovery for you and your family. Iceland is a welcoming place for families seeking unforgettable experiences with its activities suitable for all ages and stunning scenery. Join us as we explore the wonders that make Iceland the perfect backdrop for creating precious memories with your loved ones.

Taking Kids on Vacation

Bringing your family on an adventure in Iceland is like opening a book of exploration with endless possibilities for amazement, joy, and laughter. Traveling across Icelandic landscapes with children turns the journey into a series of enjoyable experiences, all carefully planned to leave lasting memories.

Following Your Family's Waterfalls

Imagine the joy in your children's eyes as you show them the wonders of Icelandic waterfalls. Like a playground in nature, the roaring cascades provide the perfect setting for a family portrait. It's not just about the waterfall; it's also about the pure delight of exploring nature's marvels together and sharing laughs.

Geysers and Nature's Dance

Exploring geysers becomes a family activity, and your children will cheer in anticipation of explosions. Imagine your youngsters marveling at the natural world's dance while the suspense grows as Strokkur launches water into the sky. It's a shared discovery moment where science and pure joy meet.

Adventures at Black Sand Beach

Walking with your family along beaches with black sand is like entering a natural playground. The children can create sandcastles, collect unusual stones, and take in the ocean's immensity. Every step on the beach is a joint investigation, turning it into a canvas for family artistic expression.

Fun with Whale Watching

Embarking on a family voyage over the Icelandic seas for whale watching is like a thrilling adventure. See the excitement in your children's eyes as they witness a magnificent whale breaching the surface. This is more than just a boat ride; it's an exploration of the underwater environment, where each splash represents shared exhilaration.

Enchanting Times in Ice Caves

Going on a family adventure into an ice cave is like stepping into a magical world. Imagine the glimmer of blue ice capturing the attention of your children. The echoes of laughter reverberate off the freezing walls of the caverns, transforming them into a mystical playground where memories shimmer like cave crystals.

Cozy Cottage Escapes for Families

Finding a family-friendly getaway in a quaint cottage is like discovering a home away from home. Before going to bed, picture the coziness of a crackling fireplace and stories shared. The cottage turns into a sanctuary where spending time with family in harmony is the real pleasure.

Together, Investigating Viking History

Learning about Viking history is like taking a family education on life. Imagine your children gazing with wide eyes as they visit historical monuments, seeing themselves transformed into fearless Viking explorers. It's more than just a history lesson; you and your family will get to see firsthand how the past and present collide.

Encamping Beneath the Icelandic Sky

Under the vast Icelandic sky, camping is like having a family overnight amid the splendor of the natural world. Imagine your children curled up under blankets, staring up at the starry sky. The simplicity of sleeping outside beneath the stars becomes the focal point of a common narrative about camping.

Icelandic family travel is more than just a holiday; it's a woven fabric of moments spent together, stories spoken, and the magic that occurs when families venture forth together. Every step you take together is a new chapter in your family's Icelandic trip, where the experience itself is the real treat, rather than just the goal. So gather your belongings, enjoy the joy of adventure, and let Iceland serve as the setting for your family's remarkable journey of discovery and camaraderie.

10 Advice for a Stress-Free Family Getaway

A family vacation in Iceland is like joining a shared adventure, where the main events are discovery, laughter, and togetherness. These simple but important suggestions, based on the real experiences of families who have visited Iceland's wonders, can help you and your loved ones have a smooth and enjoyable trip.

Dress in Layers for Icelandic Weather

Imagine getting your family ready for Iceland's changing weather by dressing them like cozy little explorers. The key to keeping everyone dry and comfortable is wearing layers. Picture your children in warm layers, waterproof coats, and snug boots, ready to face the weather with smiles on their faces.

Snack Time Adventures for Young Explorers

Turn snack time into a brief adventure by bringing a variety of treats. Imagine your children enjoying locally made snacks, skyr-flavored candies, and chocolates from Iceland. Snacking becomes a joyful family moment that provides everyone with energy for the next adventure.

Fun Learning Icelandic Phrases

Make learning Icelandic words and phrases a fun family activity. Imagine your children laughing as they try to say "Bless" for farewell or "Takk" for thank you. It's not just about words; it's about happy moments spent laughing and learning a new language together.

Capture Every Smile with a Family Camera

Bring along a simple family camera to capture every laugh and special moment. Imagine your children documenting the journey through their eyes, taking turns being the family photographer. The camera becomes a storytelling tool by capturing moments that will be cherished for years.

Treasure Hunt for Souvenirs from Iceland

Turn your family's souvenir hunt into a treasure hunt. Imagine your children eagerly searching for unique Icelandic souvenirs, like a lava rock or a small Viking ship. The souvenirs transform from tokens into actual, tangible memories of the family's treasure hunt in Iceland.

Storytime Under the Stars at Midnight

Establish a nightly routine beneath the Midnight Sun. Imagine your family sharing stories and snuggling into sleeping bags as the sun dips beyond the horizon. Combining the incredible Icelandic summer evenings with the simplicity of storytelling turns bedtime into a lovely occasion.

Embrace Regional Icelandic Food

Embrace local flavors and introduce your family to the delights of Icelandic cuisine. Imagine everyone sitting around a table enjoying traditional dishes such as fish and chips, lamb stew, or Icelandic hot dogs. Every bite becomes a celebration of Icelandic food as dining turns into a communal activity.

Journaling and Sketching Nature

Encourage your children to become little naturalists by giving them sketchbooks and diaries. Imagine them using simple notes and sketches to capture the beauty of Icelandic landscapes. Drawing nature becomes a family activity where imagination and discovery go hand in hand.

Celebrate Little Victories Together as a Family

As a family, acknowledge and celebrate each small victory, like reaching a waterfall viewpoint or successfully setting up a tent. Picture the excitement on your children's faces as they give each other high fives for overcoming a family challenge. Celebrations become the glue for your family's Icelandic journey.

These helpful tips for a stress-free family vacation in Iceland are not just practical advice; they're also invitations to create a story of special moments, laughter, and wonder from family travel. Every step you take becomes a new chapter in your family's adventure around Iceland, where happiness is found in the little things you do together rather than the final goal. So gather your belongings, embrace the thrill of adventure, and let Iceland be the backdrop for your family's remarkable journey of discovery and camaraderie.

Restaurant that allows Children

Discovering family-friendly restaurants in Iceland is like finding cozy spots where families can share happy times and meals together. These eateries go the extra mile, welcoming both parents and young children with open arms. Let's explore the unique charm of family-friendly Icelandic restaurants.

The Friendly Café with Magical Pancakes

Imagine a café where pancakes are a delightful treat, not just food. Picture the joy on your children's faces as they see stacks of pancakes topped with berries and whipped cream. This kid-friendly spot, filled with laughter and the aroma of freshly made pancakes, becomes a comforting haven.

Pizza Paradise with Playful Decor

Step into a pizza haven with playful decorations appealing to all ages. Envision your family enjoying pizza with an Icelandic twist amid vibrant colors and cartoon graphics. This pizza place transforms into a joyful retreat for the taste buds and the imagination.

Seaside Charm at the Fisherman's Wharf

Discover a fish and chips stand by the water, where the salty breeze adds to the charm. Envision your children relishing crispy fish bites while seagulls playfully circle around. Each meal at this shack brings a taste of Icelandic coastal joy, turning it into a nautical experience.

The Cozy Spot with Nordic Hot Dogs

Enter a small corner where Nordic hot dogs symbolize simplicity. Picture your family gathering at a tiny table, sharing hot dogs with locally sourced toppings. This corner becomes a meeting point where the warmth of family time blends with the joy of savoring Icelandic street cuisine.

Family-Friendly Café with Storytime Nooks

Visit a café designed for families, where fairy tales and literature come alive in Storytime corners. While sipping Icelandic coffee, imagine your children flipping through picture books. The café becomes a haven for book lovers, inviting families to unwind in an atmosphere filled with the aroma of freshly brewed coffee and the magic of storytelling.

Ice Cream Parlor with Imaginative Flavors

Indulge in ice cream from a creative parlor that sparks your curiosity. Visualize your children delighting in imaginative Icelandic ice cream creations, where each scoop carries a hint of childhood magic. The parlor transforms into a delightful haven, merging the joy of family treats with the artistry of crafting gelato.

A Delightful Restaurant with a Playful Menu
Step into a charming eatery where menus are whimsical works of art. Imagine savoring hearty Icelandic dishes while your children explore illustrated plates with their fingers. The restaurant becomes a gourmet playground where the excitement of ordering matches the thrill of the food.

Warm Bakery with Delicious Icelandic Pastries
Enter a small bakery filled with the sweet aroma of Icelandic pastries. Picture your family choosing cakes and pastries with names reminiscent of tales from traditional Icelandic culture. The bakery transforms into a decadent retreat, honoring the craftsmanship of Nordic pastry making.

In Iceland, family-friendly restaurants are more than just places to eat; they're reflections of the welcoming Icelandic culture, allowing families to enjoy the cuisine and create cherished memories along the way. These restaurants are not just dining spots; they become milestones on your family's Icelandic journey, where the joy is found in the conversations around the table as much as in the food itself. So, let your family's culinary adventures become a symphony of laughter and flavors, with each restaurant visit adding a delicious note to the overall melody of your Icelandic adventure.

CHAPTER 9

Things to do that you shouldn't miss

Get ready for an exciting journey through some of Iceland's most famous and stunning sights. We've made a list of must-see places that will grab your attention, from beautiful landscapes to hidden cultural gems.

Natural Wonders

Glaciers, Waterfalls, and Geysers

Exploring Iceland's waterfalls, glaciers, and geysers is like entering a natural paradise where the elements come alive, inviting you to appreciate the pure beauty of the place. Imagine traveling through these well-known Icelandic landmarks as a humble adventurer surrounded by the wild forces of nature.

The Breathtaking Waterfall Ballet

Imagine standing in front of a magnificent waterfall, feeling the cool mist on your face as the water gracefully descends, creating a captivating sight for your eyes. Each Icelandic waterfall has its own personality, from the powerful Gullfoss to the elegant Seljalandsfoss. It's not just about watching water move; it's joining the rhythmic dance of nature.

Encounters with Glaciers in Frozen Worlds

Picture yourself exploring Iceland's glacial areas, where the scenery is surreal due to the presence of ancient ice. Envision the vastness of the frozen landscape unfolding before you, and the crunch of snow beneath your boots as you visit glaciers like Vatnajökull. It's a journey through a frozen masterpiece shaped by time, not just a stroll on the ice.

Geysers: Nature's Steaming Marvel

Witness the steamy wonder of nature as you stand in front of a geyser. Imagine the excitement building as the geyser prepares to erupt, followed by the burst of hot water shooting upwards. Observing bubbling geothermal magic is more than witnessing a natural phenomenon; it's an experience of the earth's rhythmic pulse.

Conversations with Glacial Lagoons

Imagine having a chat with glacial lagoons, where icebergs gently float in the chilly embrace of pristine waters. Picture the icebergs at Jökulsárlón as storytellers, each sharing a tale about their journey from glacier to lagoon. It's a chance to connect with the frozen stories of Iceland's glacial past and enjoy a visual feast.

Sounds of Ice Cave Whispers

Step into the quiet ice caves, where the underground wonderland is lit by the blue hues of ancient ice. Imagine your footsteps echoing off crystalline walls as you explore caverns like Vatnajökull Ice Cave. It's a connection with the silent mysteries of Iceland's cold heart, not just a trek beneath the surface.

Hot Springs: Nature's Warm Embrace

Feel the comforting hug of nature as you soak in the geothermally heated waters of hot springs. Imagine relaxing in the Blue Lagoon or at hidden hot springs tucked away in secluded spots. It's more than just a bath; it's a chance to unwind in the cozy warmth provided by Iceland's underground fires.

Northern Lights: Heavenly Chorus in the Evening Sky

Imagine the dazzling display of colors that paints the night sky during the Northern Lights' heavenly dance. Imagine being a part of the cosmic ballet above while standing beneath the glistening curtains of light. It's a spiritual experience with the ethereal splendor of Iceland's northern evenings, not merely a visual extravaganza.

Discovering Iceland's waterfalls, glaciers, and geysers is an immersive experience that delves deeply into the essence of the country, surpassing simple tourism.

Every interaction turns into a dialogue with the natural world, a chance to step into the role of a modest player in the vast story of Iceland's geological symphony. Now pull on your boots, take in the mist on your face, and let Iceland's natural wonders—water, ice, and steam—to tell a story of breathtaking natural phenomena.

Protected Areas and National Parks

Traveling through Iceland's protected areas and national parks is like entering an outdoor sanctuary where the natural world reveals its beauties and extends an invitation for you to become a part of its narrative. See yourself as a modest participant in the living, breathing landscapes that characterize these protected zones, rather than just as a tourist.

A Historical Tapestry of Þingvellir National Park

Imagine yourself walking through a historical tapestry as you explore Þingvellir National Park. Imagine the scene of the continental drift between the North

American and Eurasian tectonic plates: picture the old Alþingi, formerly the meeting place of Viking chieftains. It's more than simply a park; it's a trip through time, with the rivers and rocks reflecting the past of Iceland.

Vatnajökull National Park: Majesty Sculpted by Glaciers

Imagine yourself in the majestic, glacier-carved surroundings of Vatnajökull National Park. Imagine the size of the largest national park in Europe, where fire and ice meet. It's a canvas created by roaring rivers, glaciers, and volcanoes, not just a landscape. The park turns into a monument to the dynamic forces that have molded Iceland's natural heritage and are still shaping it.

Wonders of the Coast and Mysterious Peaks in Snaefellsjökull National Park

Enter Snæfellsjökull National Park, a place where magical peaks and breathtaking coastlines converge.

Imagine yourself at the base of the well-known Snæfellsjökull volcano, which some people think serves as a portal to the Earth's heart. It's more than simply a park; it's an investigation into the blending of geology and mythology, with each wave and rock bearing a unique tale.

Canyon Marvels at Jökulsárgljúfur National Park
Imagine the breathtaking canyons of Jökulsárgljúfur National Park, where the powerful Jökulsá á Dal River has sculpted striking gorges into the surface of the ground. Imagine yourself trekking across Ásbyrgi's edge, enjoying the sound of birch trees rustling and the refreshing wind coming from the cliffs. It's a communion with the raw beauty that characterizes Iceland's wild landscapes, not simply a trip.

Natural Reserves: Refuges for Peace and Wildlife
Imagine these refuges as wildlife and peace havens while you explore Iceland's natural reserves. Imagine yourself exploring the natural habitats of Arctic foxes

or seabird colonies perched on isolated rocks. It's an opportunity to see the delicate balance between Iceland's distinctive flora and animals, not simply a reserve.

Safeguarding Wetlands: Lakes, Bogs, and Marshes

Imagine how important it is to preserve Iceland's wetlands, which range from peaceful lakes to bogs and marshes. Imagine yourself walking along a wetland area's boardwalks while listening to the migrating birds' sounds. It's a dedication to maintaining the essential ecosystems that sustain a wide variety of plant and animal life, not merely conservation.

Beaches, cliffs, and seals are coastal treasures.

Imagine discovering hidden coastal treasures where black sand beaches meet towering cliffs and seals lounge in the sun. Imagine yourself watching waves break against columns of basalt while standing on a windswept headland. This is more than simply a coastline—it's a front-row ticket to the dynamic drama that plays out between the sea and the land.

Discovering Iceland's protected areas and national parks is an experience that goes beyond simply taking in the scenery; it's like taking a deep dive into the country's soul. Every protected area serves as a new chapter in Iceland's continuous story, where a dedication to conservation and appreciation of the country's natural beauties foster an environment that makes every visitor feel like a custodian of the land. Therefore, let the simplicity of the landscapes and the depth of their tales lead the way as you explore these protected areas, serving as a constant reminder that in Iceland, nature is more than simply a setting—it is the main character in a constantly evolving story.

Churches, historical sites, and museums

Traveling around Iceland's museums, cathedrals, and historical monuments is like to turning the pages of a live history book, with the stunning scenery serving as a background for the telling of historical tales. Imagine yourself not just as a visitor, but also as an inquisitive nomad, ready to discover the personal anecdotes and cultural heritage that characterize these amazing locations.

Iceland's National Museum: Viking Age Treasures

Enter the National Museum of Iceland and picture yourself surrounded by Viking Age artifacts. Imagine the relics telling tales of everyday life and Norse settlement. It's more than simply a museum; it's a time-traveling experience where antique relics and finely carved items reveal the past.

A View Into Viking Life at The Settlement Exhibition

Imagine yourself in the center of Viking life at The Settlement Exhibition. Imagine yourself strolling inside a reconstruction of a Viking longhouse and sensing the echo of past discussions from these wood-framed walls. It's an interactive experience that delves into the resourcefulness and tenacity of Iceland's earliest settlers, not merely an exhibition.

Hallgrímskirkja: An Underwater Church

Present yourself in front of Hallgrímskirkja, the famous church that dominates Reykjavik's skyline. Imagine yourself standing there looking up at the towering facade, taken in by the tasteful minimalism of Icelandic design. It is more than simply a church; it is a representation of religion and the artistic energy that creates Iceland's unique architectural style.

Akureyrarkirkja: A Jewel of North Iceland

Envision coming across Akureyrarkirkja, a church tucked away in the middle of northern Iceland. Imagine yourself meandering through its calm environs, filled with colorful gardens and a peaceful atmosphere. It's a community reflection as much as a place of prayer, where spirituality melds with Iceland's stunning natural surroundings.

The Sun Voyager: Inspiration from Art and the Sea

Imagine the famous sculpture The Sun Voyager that is located along Reykjavik's shoreline. Imagine yourself standing next to this sleek steel ship, which symbolizes Iceland's maritime history and the spirit of exploration. This sculpture is more than simply a work of art; it's an artistic invitation to take a figurative voyage of your own.

Maritime Museum of Reykjavik: Tales from the Sea

Enter the Reykjavik Maritime Museum to experience the sea's tales brought to life. Imagine being surrounded by nautical memorabilia, such as old ships and stories of fearless fisherman. It's more than simply a museum; it's an exploration of Iceland's maritime past, where the tenacity of coastal towns is revealed in striking detail.

A Valley of Norse Mythology: Þórsmörk

Imagine Þórsmörk, a valley encircled by majestic mountains and rich in Norse legend. Imagine yourself strolling through settings that are reminiscent of the old sagas, with an eerie sense of Thor the thunder god's presence. It's a living canvas where myth and nature collide, not simply a valley.

Skógar Folk Museum: Ancient Customs

Imagine seeing the Skógar Folk Museum, which preserves ancient Icelandic customs. Imagine yourself strolling among relics and turf huts that narrate stories of rural life. It's a celebration of heritage, where the traditions of bygone eras are treasured and passed down, rather than just your average folk museum.

Discovering Iceland's ancient buildings, museums, and churches is more than simply a sightseeing excursion—it's an opportunity to dive into the heart of a country fashioned by its natural beauty, resiliency, and rich cultural diversity. Every location becomes a chapter in Iceland's continuous story, in which the landscapes themselves serve as a thread connecting the past and present. Therefore, let your investigation be guided by the warmth of Icelandic culture and the simplicity of its history, which will serve as a constant reminder that the stories of Iceland's past are not relics but rather live echoes that may be heard in every stone, church, and item.

Icelandic Mythology and Folklore

Taking a trip to discover Icelandic mythology and folklore is like traveling into a world where magic and reality collide. Consider yourself involved in a live narrative that has been passed down through the years, rather than just a spectator. Imagine the fantastical creatures and folktales come to life against the backdrop of Iceland's varied terrain.

Imagine the Hidden Folk and elves—ethereal inhabitants said to reside in rocks and obscure areas of the terrain—as magical inhabitants of the landscape.

Imagine yourself strolling through lava fields covered in moss, where tales of these otherworldly creatures meld well with the surrounding environment. It is more than simply folklore; it is a cultural fabric ingrained in Icelandic awareness, where reverence for the natural world coexists with the conviction that there are invisible neighbors.

The Huldufólk: The Unseen People of Iceland

As you explore isolated slopes and peaceful glades, picture yourself coming across the Huldufólk, Iceland's invisible people. Imagine the magically colored air, the place these mysterious beings are rumored to inhabit. It's more than simply mythology; it's an understanding that the invisible is a harmonic dance between the real and the other, permeating both the Icelandic environment and the apparent.

Trolls: Keepers of Hard Terrain

Imagine trolls—fabled creatures that watch over untamed areas and jagged cliff faces. Imagine these enormous giants from myth standing in front of towering cliffs or columns of basalt. It's a cultural narrative that turns geological formations into people with rich histories, reminding us that every rock has a story to tell. It's not simply stories about giants.

The Álfaborg: The Eastern Elf City

Imagine the legendary Elf City in the East, Álfaborg, where elves are rumored to be especially prevalent. Imagine yourself discovering the serene splendor of East Iceland, a place where nature and folklore meet. It's an understanding that the landscapes themselves are storytellers and that each hill, fjord, and meadow has a link to the invisible worlds. It's more than simply a destination.

The Yule Lads and the Grúla: Wintertime Folktale Treasures

Enter the world of winter legend with Grýla and the Yule Lads, two cheeky figures that make appearances around Christmas. Imagine the happiness and good humor that permeate Icelandic homes as families tell stories about these fascinating creatures. Stories of lighthearted mischief enliven the winter gloom, and it's more than simply a fun tradition—it's a cultural festival that unites communities.

Nordic Mythology: Deities and Stories

Imagine immersing yourself in Norse mythology, where stories from Iceland are weaved with the likes of Odin, Thor, and Freyja. Imagine yourself in front of scenes that evoke the heroic tales of the past. Stories of gods and legends are passed down like heirlooms through the centuries, and they represent more than simply old folklore. They represent a live link to the origins of Icelandic identity.

The Valkyries: Battlefield Maidens

Imagine the Valkyries, the legendary maidens who select the soldiers who have died for Valhalla. Imagine the coastal cliffs and windswept fields that these warrior ghosts are rumored to prowl. It's a cultural statement of bravery and valor, where the echoes of bygone conflicts remain in the very air you breathe. It's not just folklore from the battlefield.

Examining Icelandic mythology and folklore is an invitation to participate in a dynamic story that is still shaping Icelandic culture, not only a search for historical tales. Every meeting with fabled creatures, elves, trolls, and secret folk turns into a dialogue with the land's spirit, where tales aren't limited to books but instead reverberate in the whisper of the winds, the rustling of leaves, and the everlasting beauty of Iceland's magical regions. Thus, let your imagination run wild as you travel through these folklore-rich landscapes and let the legends to accompany you on your journey through Iceland's enchanted interior.

CHAPTER 10

Things to do that you shouldn't miss

As you click through this section, prepare yourself for an adventure through some of the most famous and spectacular sights in the nation. We've put together a list of must-see sights that will captivate you, ranging from breathtaking scenery to hidden cultural treasures.

Natural Enchantments

Glaciers, waterfalls, and geysers

Going on an expedition to discover Iceland's waterfalls, glaciers, and geysers is like stepping into a natural paradise where the elements come to life and beckon you to take in the unadulterated beauty of the place. Imagine yourself traveling through these well-known Icelandic landmarks as a modest adventurer surrounded by the wild powers of nature.

The Stunning Waterfall Dance

Picture yourself in front of a magnificent waterfall, enjoying the cold mist on your face while the water falls gracefully, creating a visual spectacle for your eyes. Every Icelandic waterfall has an individual character, ranging from the mighty Gullfoss to the graceful Seljalandsfoss. It's more than simply watching water move; it's joining the balletic symphony of nature.

Meetings with Glaciers in Frozen Realms

Imagine yourself exploring the glacial regions of Iceland, where the scenery is surreal due to the presence of old ice. Imagine the vastness of the frozen expanse stretched before you, and the crunch of snow beneath your boots, as you explore glaciers like Vatnajökull. It's a voyage through a frozen work of art that has been shaped by time, not merely a stroll on the ice.

Geysers: The Steaming Wonder of Nature

Witness the sultry sight of nature as you stand in front of a geyser. Imagine the excitement rising as the geyser gets ready to explode, followed by the blast of hot water that shoots upwards. Witnessing bubbling geothermal magic is more than just taking in a natural phenomenon—it's an experience of the earth's cyclic heartbeat.

Talks with the Glacial Lagoons

Envision conversing with glacial lagoons, where icebergs gently drift in the chilly embrace of immaculate waters. Imagine the icebergs at Jökulsárlón as storytellers, each one telling a tale about their journey from glacier to lagoon. It's an opportunity to connect with the frozen narratives of Iceland's glacial past as well as a visual feast.

The Sounds of Ice Cave Whispers

Enter the hushed ice caves, where underground wonderland is illuminated by the blue tones of the old ice. Imagine your footfall echoing off crystalline walls when you explore caverns such as Vatnajökull Ice Cave. It is a connection with the silent mysteries of Iceland's cold heart, not merely a trek under the surface.

Hot Springs: A Cozy Welcome from Nature

Feel the comforting embrace of nature as you submerge yourself in the geothermally heated waters of hot springs. Imagine unwinding in the Blue Lagoon or at the hidden hot springs tucked away in secluded settings. It's more than simply a bath; it's an opportunity to relax in the cozy warmth provided by Iceland's underground fires.

Northern Lights: Heavenly Chorus in the Evening Sky

Imagine the dazzling display of colors that paints the night sky during the Northern Lights' heavenly dance. Imagine being a part of the cosmic ballet above while standing beneath the glistening curtains of light. It's a spiritual experience with the ethereal splendor of Iceland's northern evenings, not merely a visual extravaganza.

Discovering Iceland's waterfalls, glaciers, and geysers is an immersive experience that delves deeply into the essence of the country, surpassing simple tourism. Every interaction turns into a dialogue with the natural world, a chance to step into the role of a modest player in the vast story of Iceland's geological symphony. Now pull on your boots, take in the mist on your face, and let Iceland's natural wonders—water, ice, and steam—to tell a story of breathtaking natural phenomena.

Protected Areas and National Parks

Traveling through Iceland's protected areas and national parks is like entering an outdoor sanctuary where the natural world reveals its beauties and extends an invitation for you to become a part of its narrative. See yourself as a modest participant in the living, breathing landscapes that characterize these protected zones, rather than just as a tourist.

A Historical Tapestry of Þingvellir National Park

Imagine yourself walking through a historical tapestry as you explore Þingvellir National Park. Imagine the scene of the continental drift between the North American and Eurasian tectonic plates: picture the old Alþingi, formerly the meeting place of Viking chieftains. It's more than simply a park; it's a trip through time, with the rivers and rocks reflecting the past of Iceland.

Vatnajökull National Park: Majesty Sculpted by Glaciers

Imagine yourself in the majestic, glacier-carved surroundings of Vatnajökull National Park. Imagine the size of the largest national park in Europe, where fire and ice meet. It's a canvas created by roaring rivers, glaciers, and volcanoes, not just a landscape. The park turns into a monument to the dynamic forces that have molded Iceland's natural heritage and are still shaping it.

Wonders of the Coast and Mysterious Peaks in Snaefellsjökull National Park

Enter Snæfellsjökull National Park, a place where magical peaks and breathtaking coastlines converge. Imagine yourself at the base of the well-known Snæfellsjökull volcano, which some people think serves as a portal to the Earth's heart. It's more than simply a park; it's an investigation into the blending of geology and mythology, with each wave and rock bearing a unique tale.

Canyon Marvels at Jökulsárgljúfur National Park

Imagine the breathtaking canyons of Jökulsárgljúfur National Park, where the powerful Jökulsá á Dal River has sculpted striking gorges into the surface of the ground. Imagine yourself trekking across Ásbyrgi's edge, enjoying the sound of birch trees rustling and the refreshing wind coming from the cliffs. It's a communion with the raw beauty that characterizes Iceland's wild landscapes, not simply a trip.

Natural Reserves: Refuges for Peace and Wildlife
Imagine these refuges as wildlife and peace havens while you explore Iceland's natural reserves. Imagine yourself exploring the natural habitats of Arctic foxes or seabird colonies perched on isolated rocks. It's an opportunity to see the delicate balance between Iceland's distinctive flora and animals, not simply a reserve.

Safeguarding Wetlands: Lakes, Bogs, and Marshes
Imagine how important it is to preserve Iceland's wetlands, which range from peaceful lakes to bogs and marshes. Imagine yourself walking along a wetland area's boardwalks while listening to the migrating birds' sounds. It's a dedication to maintaining the essential ecosystems that sustain a wide variety of plant and animal life, not merely conservation.

Beaches, cliffs, and seals are coastal treasures.

Imagine discovering hidden coastal treasures where black sand beaches meet towering cliffs and seals lounge in the sun. Imagine yourself watching waves break against columns of basalt while standing on a windswept headland. This is more than simply a coastline—it's a front-row ticket to the dynamic drama that plays out between the sea and the land.

Discovering Iceland's protected areas and national parks is an experience that goes beyond simply taking in the scenery; it's like taking a deep dive into the country's soul. Every protected area serves as a new chapter in Iceland's continuous story, where a dedication to conservation and appreciation of the country's natural beauties foster an environment that makes every visitor feel like a custodian of the land. Therefore, let the simplicity of the landscapes and the depth of their tales lead the way as you explore these protected areas, serving as a constant reminder that in Iceland, nature is more than simply a setting—it is the main character in a constantly evolving story.

Churches, historical sites, and museums

Traveling around Iceland's museums, cathedrals, and historical monuments is like to turning the pages of a live history book, with the stunning scenery serving as a background for the telling of historical tales. Imagine yourself not just as a visitor, but also as an inquisitive nomad, ready to discover the personal anecdotes and cultural heritage that characterize these amazing locations.

Iceland's National Museum: Viking Age Treasures

Enter the National Museum of Iceland and picture yourself surrounded by Viking Age artifacts. Imagine the relics telling tales of everyday life and Norse settlement. It's more than simply a museum; it's a time-traveling experience where antique relics and finely carved items reveal the past.

A View Into Viking Life at The Settlement Exhibition

Imagine yourself in the center of Viking life at The Settlement Exhibition. Imagine yourself strolling inside a reconstruction of a Viking longhouse and sensing the echo of past discussions from these wood-framed walls. It's an interactive experience that delves into the resourcefulness and tenacity of Iceland's earliest settlers, not merely an exhibition.

Hallgrímskirkja: An Underwater Church

Present yourself in front of Hallgrímskirkja, the famous church that dominates Reykjavik's skyline. Imagine yourself standing there looking up at the towering facade, taken in by the tasteful minimalism of Icelandic design. It is more than simply a church; it is a representation of religion and the artistic energy that creates Iceland's unique architectural style.

Akureyrarkirkja: A Jewel of North Iceland

Envision coming across Akureyrarkirkja, a church tucked away in the middle of northern Iceland. Imagine yourself meandering through its calm environs, filled with colorful gardens and a peaceful atmosphere. It's a community reflection as much as a place of prayer, where spirituality melds with Iceland's stunning natural surroundings.

The Sun Voyager: Inspiration from Art and the Sea

Imagine the famous sculpture The Sun Voyager that is located along Reykjavik's shoreline. Imagine yourself standing next to this sleek steel ship, which symbolizes Iceland's maritime history and the spirit of exploration. This sculpture is more than simply a work of art; it's an artistic invitation to take a figurative voyage of your own.

Maritime Museum of Reykjavik: Tales from the Sea

Enter the Reykjavik Maritime Museum to experience the sea's tales brought to life. Imagine being surrounded by nautical memorabilia, such as old ships and stories of fearless fisherman. It's more than simply a museum; it's an exploration of Iceland's maritime past, where the tenacity of coastal towns is revealed in striking detail.

Þórsmörk: A Valley of Norse Mythology

Imagine Þórsmörk, a valley encircled by majestic mountains and rich in Norse legend. Imagine yourself strolling through settings that are reminiscent of the old sagas, with an eerie sense of Thor the thunder god's presence. It's a living canvas where myth and nature collide, not simply a valley.

Skógar Folk Museum: Time-Tested Traditions

Imagine seeing the Skógar Folk Museum, which preserves ancient Icelandic customs. Imagine yourself strolling among relics and turf huts that narrate stories of rural life. It's a celebration of heritage, where the traditions of bygone eras are treasured and passed down, rather than just your average folk museum.

Discovering Iceland's ancient buildings, museums, and churches is more than simply a sightseeing excursion—it's an opportunity to dive into the heart of a country fashioned by its natural beauty, resiliency, and rich cultural diversity. Every location becomes a chapter in Iceland's continuous story, in which the landscapes themselves serve as a thread connecting the past and present. Therefore, let your investigation be guided by the warmth of Icelandic culture and the simplicity of its history, which will serve as a constant reminder that the stories of Iceland's past are not relics but rather live echoes that may be heard in every stone, church, and item.

Icelandic Mythology and Folklore

Taking a trip to discover Icelandic mythology and folklore is like traveling into a world where magic and reality collide. Consider yourself involved in a live narrative that has been passed down through the years, rather than just a spectator. Imagine the fantastical creatures and folktales come to life against the backdrop of Iceland's varied terrain.

Imagine the Hidden Folk and elves—ethereal inhabitants said to reside in rocks and obscure areas of the terrain—as magical inhabitants of the landscape. Imagine yourself strolling through lava fields covered in moss, where tales of these otherworldly creatures meld well with the surrounding environment. It is more than simply folklore; it is a cultural fabric ingrained in Icelandic awareness, where reverence for the natural world coexists with the conviction that there are invisible neighbors.

The Huldufólk: Iceland's Invisible Inhabitants

As you explore isolated slopes and peaceful glades, picture yourself coming across the Huldufólk, Iceland's invisible people. Imagine the magically colored air, the place these mysterious beings are rumored to inhabit. It's more than simply mythology; it's an understanding that the invisible is a harmonic dance between the real and the other, permeating both the Icelandic environment and the apparent.

Trolls: Keepers of Hard Terrain

Imagine trolls—fabled creatures that watch over untamed areas and jagged cliff faces. Imagine these enormous giants from myth standing in front of towering cliffs or columns of basalt. It's a cultural narrative that turns geological formations into people with rich histories, reminding us that every rock has a story to tell. It's not simply stories about giants.

The Álfaborg: Elf City in the East

Imagine the legendary Elf City in the East, Álfaborg, where elves are rumored to be especially prevalent. Imagine yourself discovering the serene splendor of East Iceland, a place where nature and folklore meet. It's an understanding that the landscapes themselves are storytellers and that each hill, fjord, and meadow has a link to the invisible worlds. It's more than simply a destination.

The Grýla and the Yule Lads: Winter Folklore Delights

Enter the world of winter legend with Grýla and the Yule Lads, two cheeky figures that make appearances around Christmas. Imagine the happiness and good humor that permeate Icelandic homes as families tell stories about these fascinating creatures. Stories of lighthearted mischief enliven the winter gloom, and it's more than simply a fun tradition—it's a cultural festival that unites communities.

Norse Mythology: Gods and Legends

Imagine immersing yourself in Norse mythology, where stories from Iceland are weaved with the likes of Odin, Thor, and Freyja. Imagine yourself in front of scenes that evoke the heroic tales of the past. Stories of gods and legends are passed down like heirlooms through the centuries, and they represent more than simply old folklore. They represent a live link to the origins of Icelandic identity.

The Valkyries: Battlefield Maidens

Imagine the Valkyries, the legendary maidens who select the soldiers who have died for Valhalla. Imagine the coastal cliffs and windswept fields that these warrior ghosts are rumored to prowl. It's a cultural statement of bravery and valor, where the echoes of bygone conflicts remain in the very air you breathe. It's not just folklore from the battlefield.

Examining Icelandic mythology and folklore is an invitation to participate in a dynamic story that is still shaping Icelandic culture, not only a search for historical tales. Every meeting with fabled creatures, elves, trolls, and secret folk turns into a dialogue with the land's spirit, where tales aren't limited to books but instead reverberate in the whisper of the winds, the rustling of leaves, and the everlasting beauty of Iceland's magical regions. Thus, let your imagination run wild as you travel through these folklore-rich landscapes and let the legends to accompany you on your journey through Iceland's enchanted interior.

CHAPTER 11

Getting Around Icelandic Cities

Get ready to experience the pulsating heart of Icelandic life as we enter metropolitan settings surrounded by breathtaking natural beauty. This chapter serves as your guide to the distinct charm, culture, and friendliness that characterize the cities of this North Atlantic jewel, from the capital city of Reykjavik to little settlements that resound with historical tales.

Seeing Reykjavik

Discovering Reykjavik is an adventure into the cultural, historical, and social fabric that creates the city's distinct identity—it goes beyond idyllic descriptions. Discover the layers that elevate Reykjavik beyond its breathtaking scenery as we explore its instructive subtleties.

Revealing the Past: Reykjavik's Viking Heritage

Imagine tracing the city's roots back to its founding in the 9th century by the Norse chieftain Ingólfur Arnarson. Reykjavik's name itself testifies to its Viking past, translating to "Smoky Bay." It is more than simply a city; it is a dynamic representation of Iceland's Viking past.

Imagine yourself in Þingvellir National Park, the site of the establishment of the Icelandic Alþingi (Parliament) in 930 AD. This is the place where democracy began. Imagine the old assembly place, where governing bodies convened to enact laws and resolve conflicts. Not only is it a park, but it's also the site of one of the oldest legislative systems in the world.

Imagine submerging yourself in the geothermal marvels of the Blue Lagoon—a hub for relaxation and a geothermal marvel. Imagine that the mineral-rich waters, drawn from a local power plant, provide visitors with more than simply a spa experience—they give a window into Iceland's resourcefulness and creativity. It's a combination of nature, sustainability, and wellbeing—it's more than simply a lagoon.

Think of Harpa Concert Hall as more than just an architectural wonder when you consider it as a modern architectural and cultural hub. Imagine it as Reykjavik's cultural center, the site of conferences, concerts, and other events. It's a vibrant place where art, creativity, and community come together—it's not just a hall.

The Literary Heritage of Reykjavik: A UNESCO City of Literature: Picture Reykjavik as more than simply a city—it's a UNESCO City of Literature. Imagine a town where there is a strong heritage of storytelling, a large number of bookstores, and an enthusiasm for words, all signs of the flourishing literature. Not only is it an honorific, but it also signifies Reykjavik's dedication to fostering the literary arts.

Beyond Skyr and Fermented Shark: Imagine Reykjavik as a center of culinary innovation, surpassing the cliches of skyr and fermented shark. Imagine the varied culinary culture of the city, where creative chefs combine traditional Icelandic ingredients with inspiration from across the world. It's a gastronomic journey that captures the multicultural character of Reykjavik, not just local cuisine.

Sustainability in Practice: The Green Initiatives of Reykjavik

Imagine Reykjavik as a sustainable leader. Imagine the city's dedication to eco-friendly policies, trash minimization, and renewable energy sources. It's more than simply a municipality; it's an example of sustainable urban living that shows how a city may coexist peacefully with the environment.

Reykjavik's Creative Scene: Design Districts and Street Art: Picture Reykjavik's design districts buzzing with creativity and its streets covered in colorful murals. Imagine living in a city that values creativity, the arts, and individual expression. It's an investigation of Reykjavik's dynamic cultural scene rather than merely a work of art.

A visit to Reykjavik invites one to interact with its story, which spans from the city's Viking beginnings to its contemporary sustainability, literary legacy, and vibrant creative scene. Every element exposes a different facet of the city's character, transforming it from a destination to a complex experience that goes beyond the descriptive words' depicted visual appeal. Explore Reykjavik's past, present, and future as you go, as every corner you turn becomes a new chapter in the dynamic tale of Iceland's largest city.

Entertainment and Nightlife Options

Entering Iceland's nightlife scene is like walking into a vibrant cultural tapestry full with tales and excitement. Iceland's evenings provide a colorful tapestry of entertainment, music, and social events in addition to its breathtaking scenery and historically significant sites. Let's explore the venues, customs, and sense of community that make Icelandic nightlife distinctive as we dig into its educative and humanized facets.

Pub Culture in Reykjavik: Looking Past the Façade

Pub culture in Reykjavik is more than simply a way to spend a night out; it's ingrained in Icelandic society as a social ritual. Picture yourself meandering through the alleyways of Laugavegur and coming across quaint bars where the residents congregate for "póst-ers"—after-work beverages. It's a social activity that promotes connections and helps people decompress from the stresses of the day, not simply drinking.

Live Music: The Pulse of the Nights in Reykjavik

Imagine Reykjavik as a center for live music, with beats resonating throughout the entire city. Imagine that both international performers and local stars will be present at small venues like as Gaukurinn and Húrra. This is more than simply a concert—it's an exploration of Iceland's musical environment, encompassing both modern and traditional sounds.

Icelandic Nights of Folklore: Tales by the Fire

Envision spending a cozy evening by a fire at a customary Icelandic storytelling gathering. Imagine the stories passed down through the decades about trolls, elves, and sagas told by the locals. This isn't simply a folklore night; it's a dynamic story that captures the spirit of timeless Icelandic storytelling.

Chasing the Northern Lights: A Celestial Show

Imagine spending a night beneath the Northern Lights, far from the lights of the city. Imagine both residents and tourists coming together to see the ethereal show that is the auroras' captivating dance. It's more than simply a natural occurrence—it's a shared experience that inspires wonder and unites people under the stars at night.

Midnight Sun Festival: Never-Ending Daytime Fun

Imagine the special Midnight Sun event that takes place in the summer. Imagine the 24-hour music marathons that festivals like Secret Solstice provide, with locals enjoying the endless daylight. It's more than simply a festival; it's evidence of Iceland's ability to adapt to harsh environmental circumstances, where evenings give way to happy celebrations throughout the day.

Hot Springs After Dark: Moonlit Swims Under the Stars

Picture yourself relaxing in Iceland's geothermal hot springs while stargazing. Imagine the peaceful but sociable ambiance as residents and guests exchange anecdotes amid the comforting warmth. It's more than simply a hot spring; it's a soothing nightly ritual that welcomes the healing power of nature.

Café Culture: Literary Evenings and Thoughtful Discussions

Imagine Reykjavik's café culture to last all night, well into afternoons when you're too tired from caffeine. Imagine places like Mokka Kaffi holding literary events and thought-provoking conversations. It's more than simply a café; it's a place where creativity is encouraged, ideas blossom, and literature comes to life at night.

The nightlife of Iceland goes beyond the typical description, providing a diverse range of community, natural, and cultural activities. Let each location and custom you experience throughout your nights in Reykjavik serve as a chapter in a constantly changing story that highlights the city's vibrant after-dark culture. It's more than just a night out—it's a chance to learn about Icelandic culture, celebrate diversity, and dance under the stars or under the Midnight Sun.

Festivals of Music

Discovering Reykjavik's music festival scene is like to losing yourself in a melodic symphony where the beats are in tune with Iceland's distinct vitality. Reykjavik's music festivals weave a lively tapestry of sounds that transcend the city's scenic landscapes and ancient monuments, encouraging artistic expression, celebration, and a sense of community. Let's explore the humanized and educative facets of Reykjavik's music festivals, dissecting the legends, customs, and cultural importance that give each occasion a unique feel.

Icelandic Airwaves: A Sonoran Investigation of Variety

Envision Iceland Airwaves, a yearly music celebration that turns Reykjavik into a refuge for music lovers. Imagine tiny pubs and venues like Harpa Concert Hall playing home to a varied roster of well-known international performers as well as up-and-coming local performers. It's a musical trip that reflects the diverse nature of Reykjavik's music culture, not just a festival.

Uncovered Solstice: Honoring the Midnight Sun

Imagine Secret Solstice, a celebration that takes place on the summer solstice beneath the hypnotic warmth of the Midnight Sun. Imagine people having a grand time in the light of day, with stages situated against the stunning scenery of Iceland. It's a celebration of nature's marvels, not simply a music festival, with celebrations that never really end when the sun sets.

Reykjavik Jazz Festival: Notes That Echo Through the Fjords: Picture yourself at the Reykjavik Jazz Festival, where the sound of jazz music permeates the city, fostering a sense of rhythm and improvisation. Imagine small, outdoor settings and areas with jazz virtuosos performing, encouraging a love of this music. It's a celebration of musical diversity rather than merely a festival, encouraging listeners to delve into the subtleties of jazz in a northern context.

Imagine the Iceland Folk Festival, a festival of folk music-based storytelling, where stories are told via strings and vocals. Imagine artists maintaining Iceland's ancient storytelling traditions by narrating stories with voice and music. It's more than simply a musical performance; it's a cultural excursion, with every melody serving as a link between the audience and the folklore of the nation.

Dark Music Days: An Exploration of Experimental Sounds: Picture yourself attending Dark Music Days, a cutting-edge event that examines modern compositions and experimental sounds. Imagine spaces like Nordurljos in Harpa, where performances that push the frontiers of music are held. This is more than simply a festival; it's an immersive event that invites participants to delve into the undiscovered realms of sound design.

Reykjavik Arts Festival: A interdisciplinary Event Where Music Converges with Other Art Forms: Envision the Reykjavik Arts Festival as an interdisciplinary gathering. Imagine performers, visual artists, and musicians working together to create a multisensory experience. It's more than simply a music festival; it's an occasion to celebrate how the arts are intertwined and to invite viewers to get fully immersed in a creative synthesis.

Visualize the LungA Art Festival as an intimate meeting place for new sounds and an artist community.

LungA Art Festival: Community, Creativity, and new Sounds. Imagine performances taking place in unusual locations throughout Seydisfjordur, fostering an environment where imagination is unrestricted. It's a grassroots movement that promotes artistic expression and community development, not merely a music festival.

Imagine Aldrei fór ég suður as an anti-festival in Ísafjörður where out-of-the-ordinary acts take center stage. This is Aldrei fór ég suður. Imagine both residents and tourists appreciating the raw beauty of spontaneous performances in unusual settings. It's more than simply a festival—it's an anti-conventional celebration of music in its unadulterated, unprocessed state.

Music festivals in Reykjavik are more than just entertainment; they tell cultural tales via the use of melodies, rhythms, and group collaborations. Take in the sounds of these events as if every note were a new chapter in the tale of Icelandic music, showcasing the creativity, diversity, and sense of community that characterize Reykjavik's dynamic musical scene.

Past Reykjavik

Traveling outside of Reykjavik reveals a mosaic of quaint cities and seaside communities, each with a distinct history carved into the untamed Icelandic terrain. Let's explore the educational and humane features of these places as we travel around these lovely areas, learning about their rich histories, diverse cultures, and welcoming local populations.

Akureyri: The Northern Capital

Envision Akureyri, tucked away in the breathtaking Eyjafjörður fjord. Imagine the famous Akureyrarkirkja church, botanical gardens, and streets dotted with vibrant homes. It's the capital of the North, not simply a town, with thriving cultural scene, home to the annual Akureyri Art Festival, and a window into life outside of Iceland's busy city.

Picture the town of Stykkishólmur, which is located on the Snæfellsnes Peninsula and has quirky charms while offering a view of Breiðafjörður Bay. Imagine the well-known port, with its vibrant homes and the expansive vista from the town's hill. It is more than simply a charming beach town—it is a center of culture that is home to the Norwegian House and features artwork by regional artists.

Ísafjörður: The Westfjords' Capital

Imagine the vibrant capital of the Westfjords, Ísafjörður. Imagine a town with striking fjords and mountains all around it, surrounded by old structures such as the Westfjords Heritage Museum that serve as reminders of Iceland's maritime history. It's more than simply a seaside community; it's the entry point to the wild splendor of the Westfjords, beckoning discovery and cross-cultural interaction.

Húsavík: The Center for Whale Watching

Consider Húsavík, well known as Iceland's whale-watching capital. Imagine the charming harbor at Skjálfandi Bay, where boats cruise to meet friendly giants. It's more than simply a seaside town; it's evidence of how community and environment can coexist, with whale sightings becoming a pleasant aspect of daily life.

Seyðisfjörður: An Adorable East Coast Haven

Picture the town of Seyðisfjörður in the Eastfjords, tucked away in a beautiful fjord and encircled by snow-capped mountains. Imagine the LungA Art Festival bringing to life the vibrant cultural scene, the recognizable blue church, and the bright wooden cottages. It's an artistic retreat where creativity blossoms against a backdrop of natural beauty, not merely a beach sanctuary.

Grundarfjörður: Kirkjufell's Majesty framed it

Imagine the village of Grundarfjörður, surrounded by the towering Kirkjufell mountain. Imagine the port, with its distinctive peak serving as the background behind which fishing boats bob. Beyond merely a seaside community, Snæfellsnes Peninsula welcomes outdoor enthusiasts to experience some of Iceland's most breathtaking scenery.

Siglufjörður: North Coast Mountains Embracing

Envision Siglufjörður, a village on the northern shore surrounded by mountains. Imagine the picturesque port, the Herring Era Museum, and the breathtaking landscape that make up this treasure of the north. More than merely a seaside community, it offers a window into Iceland's industrial past, when the locals' way of life was influenced by herring.

Djúpivogur: The Meeting Point of Art and Nature

Imagine the east coast village of Djúpivogur, where art and nature coexist together. Imagine the well-known

Eggs of Merry Bay, an outdoor sculpture installation that honors many bird species seen in the area. It's more than simply a seaside hamlet; it's an outdoor gallery where the surrounding landscape is incorporated into the art.

Traveling outside of Reykjavik reveals a mosaic of quaint cities and seaside communities, each with its own distinct personality and cultural importance. Allow the rich history, the friendliness of the locals, and the breathtaking scenery to become parts of your Icelandic adventure as you visit these places, providing a deeper insight into life outside of the city.

CHAPTER 12

Local Iceand Experiences

Taking part in local activities in Iceland is a chance to get below the surface and truly feel the pulse of the nation. We dive into the core of Icelandic culture, creating lasting relationships and having a beneficial effect on both tourists and the environment as we investigate ways to interact with people, take part in environmentally conscious excursions, and appreciate the creativity of regional handicrafts and mementos.

Making Friends, Crossing Cultural Divides, Telling Tales: Imagine the warmth of getting to know people in busy areas or little villages. Imagine having sincere discussions, exchanging anecdotes over a cup of coffee, and learning about the subtleties of Icelandic life. It's a chance to build bridges across cultures, promote understanding, and leave enduring memories of shared experiences—it's more than just a cultural exchange.

Farmstays & Homestays: Taking Hospitality to Heart

Imagine the genuineness of farmstays or homestays, where visitors integrate with the community. Imagine taking part in everyday activities, enjoying delicious Icelandic cuisine, and waking up to the sounds of nature. More than just a place to stay, it's a gateway to authentic Icelandic hospitality, where guests are welcomed as honorary locals.

Eco-Friendly Tours: Conscientiously Investigating

Nature Imagine green trips that go beyond traditional tourism. Imagine tours that are guided by informed residents who place a high value on protecting the environment. This trip is more than simply a sightseeing excursion; it's an educational experience that teaches visitors how to minimize their environmental impact and adopt sustainable habits while taking in the stunning scenery of Iceland.

Local Project Participation in Community-Led Initiatives: Envision taking part in community-driven campaigns, such as cultural preservation or beach clean-ups. Imagine helping local environmental projects and efforts to preserve Iceland's distinctive cultural heritage. It's an opportunity to actively connect with local communities and make a good influence on the areas you visit, not merely volunteer work.

Culinary Traditions: Sharing Meals and Tasting Experiences: Imagine eating at places other than restaurants, where people invite visitors to partake in customary meals. Imagine mastering the art of cooking traditional Icelandic cuisine, knowing the history behind each recipe, and relishing the tastes of regional ingredients. It's a celebration of culinary heritage and a chance to bond around shared culinary experiences, not simply a meal.

Customized Workshops: Specializing in Regional Crafts

Envision conventional work spaces where skilled workers impart centuries-old techniques. Imagine receiving one-on-one instruction from proficient locals in pottery-making, detailed pattern carving, or knitting wool from Iceland. It's an immersion into the craftsmanship that characterizes Icelandic culture, not simply a workshop, creating a concrete link to the nation's artistic past.

Local Markets: Investigating Handcrafted Treasures

Imagine exploring neighborhood marketplaces and finding one-of-a-kind items created by regional craftspeople. Imagine colorful displays of handcrafted products that capture the essence of Icelandic workmanship, such as jewelry and woolen goods. It's more than simply a market; it's an exhibition of creativity where visitors may help small businesses in the area and bring a little of Icelandic culture with them.

Festivals and Festivities: Taking Part in Local Celebrations Consider attending regional events that foster community unity, such as festivals and celebrations. Imagine taking part in live music performances, dancing the traditional way, and soaking up the festive spirit of Iceland. It's an invitation to join the shared spirit that characterizes communal life in Iceland, not merely an event.

Accepting local experiences in Iceland is a call to go beyond the role of tourist; it's a chance to integrate temporarily into a community, learn about the nuances of everyday life, and make a good impact on the areas you visit. By making connections with the locals, practicing eco-friendliness, and appreciating the creativity of regional crafts, you become a part of Icelandic culture and leave a lasting impression that goes beyond the confines of a standard tourist encounter.

CONCLUSION

We hope that reading through the in-depth chapters of this travel book has piqued your interest and feeling of anticipation for the delights that lie ahead on this unique island as your Icelandic adventure unfolds through its pages. Iceland invites with wide arms, providing not only a location but a holistic experience that goes beyond traditional travel, from the gushing waterfalls to the complex cultural tapestry.

Explore this country's fascinating past, where epic tales are told against the stunning backdrop of its natural surroundings. Sensate the pulse of the land, sculpted by age-old customs that have persisted till the present day and by volcanic forces. Iceland's past is more than just a history book; it is a story embedded in every fjord, every rock, and every kind grin on the faces of its kind people.

Choose the right time to come based on the weather and discover the captivating dance of the Northern Lights or the everlasting sunshine of the Midnight Sun. Discover how Iceland's transportation system works to get you to the furthest corners of this island of contrasts.

With a thorough itinerary and knowledge of lodging options ranging from comfortable guesthouses to the surreal appeal of ice hotels, you can make the most of your journey. Discover the skill of selecting the ideal accommodation that embodies the essence of your visit and prepare your baggage with an understanding of pre-travel necessities.

Explore off the well-traveled routes and discover quaint cities, seaside settlements, and the center of Reykjavik, where the natural beauty and cultural diversity meet. Take in the heart-pounding energy of Icelandic music festivals, where inventiveness has no boundaries and harmonies resound across fjords.

Make deep ties with the people by interacting with them beyond your function as a guest. Take part in environmentally conscious excursions that protect Iceland's stunning scenery for future generations. Contribute to community-led projects, try regional food, and support local artists to make a lasting impression on the areas you visit.

When you get to the last pages of this guide, we encourage you to think of your trip to Iceland as a narrative that is woven into the fabric of the country rather than as a list of sites you have seen. Iceland offers an experience that will stay with you and make you want to return, whether you want to travel alone, with loved ones, on romantic vacations, or in the company of other tourists.

I hope your journey around Iceland is full with amazing, meaningful, and educational experiences. Accept the unexpected, enjoy each sunrise and sunset, and let the essence of Iceland to permeate your being. Remember that the real essence of Iceland is found in the tales it inspires in you, not only in the scenery as you say goodbye to these pages. May your Icelandic trip be as limitless as the views that unfold in front of you, brave traveler. Safe travels.